third edition
GOAL DIRECTED PROJECT MANAGEMENT

Effective Techniques and Strategies

Erling S Andersen
Kristoffer V Grude
Tor Haug

Edited by:
Mike Katagiri
Rodney Turner

KOGAN
PAGE

London and Sterling, VA

658.404

Publisher's note

Every possible effort has been made to ensure that the information contained in this book is accurate at the time of going to press, and the publishers and authors cannot accept responsibility for any errors or omissions, however caused. No responsibility for loss or damage occasioned to any person acting, or refraining from action, as a result of the material in this publication can be accepted by the editor, the publisher or any of the authors.

First published in Norway in 1984 by NKI – forlaget

Hardback edition first published in Great Britain in 1987 by Kogan Page Limited (Translated from Norwegian by Roberta Wiig)
Reprinted in paperback in 1988
Second edition 1995
Third edition 2004

120 Pentonville Road
London N1 9JN
UK
www.kogan-page.co.uk

22883 Quicksilver Drive
Sterling VA 20166–2012
USA

ISBN 0 7494 4186 0

British Library Cataloguing-in-Publication Data

A CIP record for this book is available from the British Library.

Library of Congress Cataloging-in-Publication Data

Andersen, Erling S.
  Goal directed project management : effective techniques and strategies / Erling S. Andersen, Kristoffer V. Grude, Tor Haug.-- 3rd ed. / edited by Mike Katagiri and Rodney Turner.
    p. cm.
  Rev. ed. of: Goal directed project management / Erling S. Andersen ... [et al.]. 1987.
  Includes bibliographical references.
  ISBN 0-7494-4186-0
  1. Project management. 2. Strategic planning. 3. Management by objectives. I. Grude, Kristoffer V. II. Haug, Tor. III. Katagiri, Mike. IV. Turner, J. Rodney (John Rodney), 1953- V. Goal directed project management. VI. Title.

  HD69.P75G62 2004
  658.4'04--dc22

                            2004000616

Typeset by Saxon Graphics Ltd, Derby
Printed and bound in Great Britain by Creative Print and Design (Wales), Ebbw Vale

GOAL
DIRECTED
PROJECT
MANAGEMENT

Contents

1

Introduction

This book deals with project management and presents the requirements for successful projects. We show you how to use proven methods and tools to guide your projects towards their goals, thereby significantly increasing your probability of achieving project success.

The book is written for project managers and everyone participating in projects. Throughout the book we use 'he' and related words purely for convenience. There are many female project managers and, therefore, 'she' is implied equally throughout. The book requires no special previous knowledge of project work.

Much of project literature features the technical aspects of projects such as the development of software, construction of bridges, roads, airports or oil platforms. We assert that project professionals need a broader 'PSO' perspective. PSO stands for **P**eople, **S**ystem and **O**rganization; PSO projects simultaneously develop a 'system' (for example, a physical product or object), develop people and develop the organization. Projects failing to address these objectives will find implementation difficult. Therefore it is wise for project professionals to develop a 'PSO way of thinking'. We discuss PSO projects in this chapter.

In Chapter 2 we look at characteristic features of a project and conditions that make project work a unique business process requiring special methods and tools. A discussion of these dissimilarities will aid in understanding the special management problems in project work.

We deal with conditions that we know from experience create problems in project work. We refer to these conditions as 'pitfalls'. The discussion of pitfalls in Chapter 3 further illustrates the need for special methods and tools in project work.

Against this background, Chapters 4–8 are a basic course in how to manage projects and how to use the specific methods and tools of Goal Directed Project Management (GDPM). We deal with the foundation of the project (Chapter 4), global planning (Chapter 5) and organization (Chapter 6). Thereafter we discuss detailed planning and organization (Chapter 7). Control (Chapter 8) is an integral part of project management.

We discuss ways of achieving quality in project work (Chapter 9). We look at how to create a company culture with an understanding of project work and what that implies for different categories of project participants (Chapter 10). At the end (Chapter 11) we present an example of the use of GDPM and sum up the benefits of using the methods and techniques of this project methodology.

Figure 1.1 gives a schematic presentation of GDPM. The figure shows the tools we recommend for project planning, organization and control.

Level Task	Planning	Organization	Control
Foundation of project	Project mandate Mission breakdown structure Stakeholder analysis	Principle responsibility chart	
Global level (milestone level)	Milestone plan	Project responsibility chart	Milestone report
	Uncertainty analysis		
Detail level (activity level)	Activity responsible chart		Activity report

Figure 1.1 Overview of Goal Directed Project Management

We distinguish between three levels of project work: foundation level (where the basis for the project is created and the relationships between the project and its environment are clarified), global level (where overall plans and organization are determined) and detail level (where all the different activities of the project are described).

It is of great importance to elucidate the foundation. The project mandate provides the background for the project and shows its purpose and goals. The mission breakdown structure assists in setting the boundaries of the project and defining the scope of the project and the goals precisely. Stakeholder analysis helps in understanding the needs of the many stakeholders and setting goals that appeal to them. The principle responsibility chart shows the division of work between different parties involved in managing the project, especially the responsibilities of the project and the organization providing resources to the project.

The milestone plan is a global plan for project progress, with checkpoints in the form of milestones to be achieved. The milestone responsibility chart shows the roles necessary for attaining the different milestones. An uncertainty analysis reveals elements that could make it difficult to achieve the milestones and what might be done to reduce the uncertainties. The milestone report shows where the project is in relation to the milestone plan.

The activity responsibility chart shows the specific people needed to work on the activities necessary for reaching a milestone. It also shows when the different activities must be performed. An activity report is used to show the detailed work progress supporting milestone accomplishment.

ABOUT PSO PROJECTS

PSO development is an abbreviation for development of people, system and organization. The concept was used originally within the field of information technology. It is based on countless experiences with the implementation of IT systems. These experiences taught us that successful implementation requires more than a concern with the technical development of the computer system. It must always be accompanied by planned development of the affected personnel and the organization's relationships, responsibilities and authorities. This is necessary to achieve the required benefits of systems development, and to prevent it from having negative effects on people and the organization.

When introducing a new IT system, a frequent mistake is to overemphasize the technical work. The development of people and organization necessary to enable the system to function well is either totally neglected or paid insufficient attention. The PSO concept reminds us of the importance of balancing all three elements.

We have found the PSO approach to be extremely useful in other types of project work. Projects often involve the building or installation of a physical product. It is very easy to become so preoccupied with this that the training and motivation of the people who will use this product are forgotten. It is easy to overlook the fact that innovations also facilitate completely new forms of organization.

Therefore, we use the PSO concept in project planning. The 'S', however, must be given a broad interpretation. It stands for technical aspects of the project. It often represents what we can 'touch and feel' in the project. In a product development project, the new product forms the 'S'; in a construction project, the new building is the 'S'; in a merger project, the newly merged organization is the 'S'. Using the PSO concept requires a little thought and extra effort, but the reward is a broader view of what the project involves. The need to consider people and organization is not forgotten. It forces one to think through consequences and possibilities in fields other than the purely technical.

The most common failing in project work is to focus too strongly on the technical content. In typical organizational development projects the situation is the reverse. These are solely concerned with developing people in the organization and relationships between them. There is too little emphasis on developing systems (eg work processes and procedures) which will support the changes required in the organization.

PSO projects are thus projects where the result should be a composite 'product'; goals should be achieved in all 'P', 'S' and

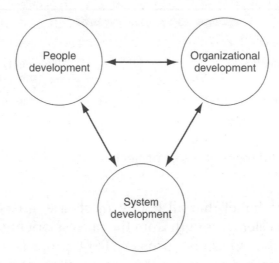

Figure 1.2 PSO project

'O'. Figure 1.2 should in its simplicity remind us of the importance of PSO.

Another important and characteristic aspect of project work is the extent to which people who will use the results are invited to participate in the work. One extreme is the purely specialist project. In such projects all the work is performed by specialists without any form of cooperation or consultation with the end users. An example may be a technical installation according to specific instructions, or an expert report by two or three technical specialists. Here there is no place for user cooperation or any opening for new approaches to problems and solutions, which may follow from cooperation with the users.

The other extreme is the purely process-oriented project. Here little or no consideration is given to planning the technical outcome. On the contrary, everyone is encouraged to become involved, and the project is allowed to be dominated by whatever problems and possibilities the participants see as being most important at any given time. The process itself (the interaction between people and what it leads to) determines the progress of the project. We have illustrated these types of projects on a scale (Figure 1.3).

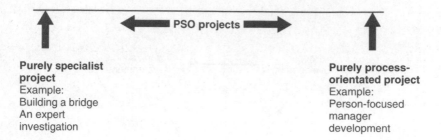

Figure 1.3 Different types of projects

It is our firm belief that all PSO projects are 'mixed' projects. They contain elements both from the process-oriented approach and from the specialist project. PSO projects often have profound consequences for the organization and the people within it. It is important that the people concerned become involved in the project and that they are given an opportunity to influence it. Their attitude towards, and understanding of, the result produced depends to a great extent on the manner in which they have participated in the project activities.

However, PSO projects can also contain complex technical elements, where a successful result depends entirely on using expertise and using methods and technology with great precision. In one and the same PSO project some activities may be very highly process oriented while others may be highly expert dominated.

GOAL DIRECTED PROJECT MANAGEMENT

This book, then, deals with the management of PSO projects. It is essential in PSO projects that there be a balance between development of the 'system' (the 'object' to be constructed) and development of people and organization. Work will typically consist of process-oriented and specialist-oriented parts.

Management consists of organizing the use of resources and the work towards goals. Both the organization and the work towards goals are complex, particularly when providing a product which is not purely technical but a composite result. In a

PSO project the deliverables consist of some technology (which may be physically inspected), but also of people with new knowledge and attitudes and of an organization and environment within which the system and the people can function well.

The responsibility for the project achieving its goals does not rest solely with the formal project manager. Everyone who can contribute in one way or another to the project achieving the desired goals is responsible for the project result.

In PSO projects goal management is absolutely essential. One must not lose sight of the composite goal. It is simpler when constructing a bridge or building a house. The goal is concrete – the bridge or the house. With PSO projects the goal is more abstract. It is easy to be preoccupied with the more concrete or technical aspects of the project, the completion date, for example, rather than with the composite goal.

In order to underline how important it is to remain continually aware of the composite goal, we have called the book and the method we present Goal Directed Project Management (GDPM).

The method contains procedures and tools that support project management. It shows how to organize resources in an organizationally complex situation. It shows how to set goals, and break each goal down into controllable intermediate goals, and how to divide work tasks into many parts and then monitor them so that the intermediate goals are achieved on the way towards a completed project.

2

Project characteristics

What is a project? In order to understand a project, consider it in the context of the organization that undertakes it. The organization can be a company, a voluntary organization or a branch of the civil service. These all aim to produce certain goods or provide services. One organization produces chocolate, another aluminium products; some organizations educate and do research; still others offer health services. Each organization is structurally tailor-made for the type of production or activity in which it engages. This means that each worker has set tasks, which must be performed repeatedly. This applies to everyone working in the organization, from those on the factory floor or the hospital ward to those who manage the organization. The manager's day is not as structured as that of the workers lower down in the hierarchy, but the manager also has set tasks, such as the development of strategy plans and budgets, preparation for board meetings, and so forth. Everyone in the organization has what we call repetitive tasks.

Now and then, however, tasks arise that the organization is not as equipped to deal with. These are tasks of a non-recurring type. They have not been done previously and will not be done again in the foreseeable future. Examples might be moving to a new location, holding an anniversary celebration or finding opportunities for entering into a new international market. Each of these tasks involves many people in the organization, yet it does not belong in any one place in the organization.

In cases like these the project approach is highly efficient and effective. It is an alternative to performing the task using the traditional organizational structure and communication. We will refer to the traditional organization as the base organization. We establish a project to carry out a defined task because the base organization is not adequately organized to perform it. The new organization is a temporary one; it will exist only until it has fulfilled its task. We call the temporary organization a project.

In Figure 2.1 we have summarized the characteristic features of a project. You will find such a list in most textbooks on project work. The description in Figure 2.1 is often used as a definition of a project. Below we make more detailed comments on the different characteristic features of a project and indicate what is important from a general management perspective.

A project
- is a unique task
- is designed to attain a specific result
- requires a variety of resources
- is limited in time

Figure 2.1 Characteristic features of a project

A UNIQUE TASK

One reason for organizing a task as a project is because it is a unique, one-time task. If it is a task that will be performed repeatedly, it is left with the base organization to perform.

The problem with a unique task is that no one has performed it previously. Therefore, at the outset one does not know in detail what activities need to be performed and consequently one does not have a detailed blueprint for how to proceed in order to achieve the desired results. An analysis must be made of what work needs to be done and in what order. Project work must therefore be planned by a method other than that used for the tasks of the base organization.

It is important to emphasize that a project task is also new to specialists – even if they have performed the same type of work previously – as it is often performed in an unfamiliar area, in a new environment and/or with new people. A person who has been a project manager for a PSO project in one organization cannot copy the activities from that project into another context. The change process to be undertaken will be different because it deals with different people in a different environment. The activities may consequently be totally different, even if they are aiming towards the same result.

A consultant may have done an excellent job as a project manager responsible for implementing a computerized salary system in an organization. However, that same consultant may not succeed in implementing the same system in another organization. Many wonder why this is so. Is it because he uses the same approach regardless of the people and the environment in which he is working? A further examination could reveal that he did not understand the importance of the 'P' and 'O' elements of the project. If so, he should have made a new plan because he was confronted with a new task.

ATTAINMENT OF A SPECIFIC RESULT

A project is established to perform a specific task in order to achieve a specific result. The task can vary greatly from project to project. One project may be to construct a bridge over a river, another the implementation of a computer system in the accounting function of an organization, a third an investigation of the consequences of moving part of an organization to another geographical location.

It is important to bear in mind that a project is formed to achieve a specific result. It is equally important to point out that there may be very different emphases on process-oriented and specialist-oriented work in order to achieve that result (see the discussion in Chapter 1). In a PSO project, the process-oriented elements are of importance. The work of developing relationships between the participants and attitudes towards the task in question is an essential part of the project.

A PSO project is a change process. It is a process that changes people's working environment as well as their understanding of the organization of which they are part. Consequently, project management is change management. It is a completely different, highly sensitive and difficult management task compared with the one that a line manager usually has. A line manager primarily manages tasks that are constantly repeated each day, week or year, and the people involved are aware of the effect of these actions.

An organization that treats project work as only specialist work causes particular problems for a PSO project manager. In such cases it may be difficult for him to obtain acceptance for the importance of the work on the process-oriented elements. Often they are the most time-consuming parts of the project.

REQUIRES A VARIETY OF RESOURCES

The temporary organization – the project – has at the outset no resources. It must receive all its resources from the permanent organization, the base organization. Particularly in organizations that are not accustomed to working with projects, it is difficult to achieve an understanding of the amount of resources required for a successful project. There are several reasons why base organizations are reluctant to commit resources:

- They hope that staff can participate in project work on top of their regular job, without any reduction in their original responsibilities.
- They do not understand why the project should take such a long time. (Perhaps because they have no firm grasp of their own use of resources.)
- They think they can negotiate a shorter time frame.
- They do not understand that a reduction in resources means a reduction in quality, and that a reduction in quality creates problems at the next stage.
- They believe that a lack of resources will resolve itself along the way.

Problems are intensified if the project is highly process oriented. It is even more difficult to gain acceptance for the time and effort required for this type of work. One can understand to a certain extent that technical work requires resources because one can see the physical processes. With process-oriented projects, however, line managers often have a limited understanding of what it takes to achieve good results. This makes it difficult to have a realistic discussion of resource requirements. (We are not saying here that all 'P' and 'O' activities necessarily take a long time. Some situations require a long period of development, but it often takes a surprisingly short time to obtain much better results. A few days of concentrated effort on the 'P' and 'O' areas, therefore, gives significant results compared with neglecting these issues.)

The second point is that even with a real understanding of the need for resources, there are often problems releasing the required people at the required time. Usually people in the base organization are committed on a full-time basis to other tasks and cannot participate in the project unless these other tasks are covered one way or another. This situation creates special management problems.

With regard to resources, most organizations are geared up for an average workload. This means that the organization is understaffed during periods with a heavy workload, while idle during 'quiet periods'. Attention should be paid to this when staffing a project.

The third management problem is that a project includes people from different backgrounds having different expertise and experience. That a project brings together people with different skills is precisely the point of project management; project tasks are solved by precisely this method. These people have probably not worked together previously and this is a challenge for the project manager. The people are not necessarily difficult to handle, but their varied backgrounds, expectations and ambitions can impede the success of a project if no effort is made to develop the team. Time must be devoted to providing opportunities for project members to get to know how to work with each other, enabling them to draw on each other's strengths later on. Also, adequate time must be invested to align team members to the goals of the project.

TIME CONSTRAINTS

A typical feature of a project is a fixed completion date. There is often a strong focus on this date and the success of the project will be judged on whether or not the project is completed by then.

A task subject to time limits is not a feature special to project work, but the focus on the completion date is stronger here than in many other cases. In the base organization with repetitive tasks there are additional opportunities to make up time if the deadline is exceeded. There is no such possibility in project work. A black shadow always hangs over a project that does not meet its deadlines.

Problems are intensified for project management if the completion date for the project is set on a fairly arbitrary basis or if only the technical aspects of the project are considered. We will discuss later how to set reasonable completion dates for projects, but we must already point out that it is psychologically unsound to connect all expectations for change to one specific date. If results have not been achieved by that date, there will likely be a sharp drop in motivation in the base organization. Alternatively, we recommend that intermediate results be planned for delivery during the course of the project. In this way, a 'big day' crisis situation is defused.

PROJECT MANAGEMENT

We have discussed above the characteristic features of a project. We have also stressed the fact that a project may surface unique leadership and management problems. Figure 2.2 is a reformula-

---

A project
- involves new and unknown tasks
- leads to changes in people's daily work or living conditions .
- might find it difficult to get the right people at the right time, and if they are available, they have different backgrounds and are not used to working together
- is subject to a strict deadline

Figure 2.2 Characteristic features of a project (reformulated)

tion of Figure 2.1. The new figure illustrates the particular problems presented by projects.

A PSO project implements change. This unto itself is inherently difficult. The change must also occur within a stated period of time. It is an unknown task for many of those involved. Resources will be required that in many cases are not available, or belong to other managers, organizationally speaking. It is not surprising that project work is a difficult task.

A project requires the establishment of an organizational structure. The work within this structure is managed with the assistance of specific methods and tools. Project management establishes the foundation for the project. It plans, organizes and controls it (see Figure 2.3).

A recipe for good project management can, of course, draw on our general knowledge of management, but the special conditions associated with project work also mean that project management requires special knowledge, methods and tools.

Project Management:
- Establish foundation for the project
- Plan project work
- Organize project work
- Control project work

Figure 2.3 Tasks in project management

3

Pitfalls in project management

There are several factors leading to the success or failure of a project. In this chapter we discuss some of the pitfalls that can occur on the road to a successful project. The pitfalls are grouped under five headings:

- foundation of the project;
- planning of the project;
- organization of the project;
- control of the project;
- execution of the project work.

The first four are about project management, and the last is about the quality of professional work being undertaken. We will focus on factors that often represent problems for the project. If we are aware of these factors, we can look for ways to avoid them.

CRACKS IN THE FOUNDATION

The project is established by the base organization. It is a challenge to make this cooperation work. The project owner is the senior executive who has the main responsibility for the project on behalf of the base organization. The relationship between the project and the project owner is essential to the project. In particular, we shall consider the degree to which the project owner supports the project. The project owner's attitude, and the preliminary work done to establish the project, provide the foundation for the project. If there are cracks in this foundation (Figure 3.1), the total project will suffer.

We first address the dangers to projects that have little or no support of the project owner or the base organization in general.

Insufficient support for the project:
- The project is not aligned with the business plans
- Stakeholders are opposed to the project
- The principles and policies of project work are not defined

Poor project definition:
- The goals for the project are imprecise
- The levels of ambition for changes to people, systems and organization are not in balance

---

Figure 3.1 Cracks in the foundation

Unaligned project and organization plans

A close correlation between the organization plans and the desired results from the project should exist. The project must fit into the overall plans of the organization. The projects goals and organizational objectives must be in harmony. Furthermore, the project's activities must be given adequate priority by the organization. Unfortunately, it is not uncommon to find project work initiated without any connection to other organization plans.

This is often true of new IT systems that can have major impacts on the people, organization and other systems. If a PSO project is not evaluated in the larger context, a conflict can easily occur between the direction in which the organization's management wants the organization to develop and the way in which the project work contributes to that development.

If a person has a good idea about a new product, would it be harmful to start a project to explore the idea further? Or is it wrong to study whether the organization should consider giving a new international market a try if the organization has many experienced sales people familiar with that marketplace? It might indeed be very negative if those are just some loose thoughts, unconnected with the organization's strategy.

If a project lacks support, there is no doubt who will be the loser in this tug of war. Neither leadership nor project management method can save a project that has little backing within the organization. A project without steady support from the top can end dramatically. When the organization's management realize that a project is heading for a collision with more important plans, they will 'pull the plug'.

However, it is more common for management to have a half-hearted attitude towards such a project. The project is then choked slowly by a lack of necessary resources and decisions. In all discussions about resources the project invariably loses owing to its lack of support. The project may continue but without the hope of reaching its original goals. People step in to do the work that should have been done by others. For example, in an IT project, programmers do jobs that should have been done by the users, because the users give insufficient priority to the project and do not provide resources for it. The result is an IT system with insufficient user input.

Securing the alignment between the long-term plans of the organization and the project is outside the treatise of this book. Methods and techniques of this book will not rescue the project if the base organization realizes that the project pulls the organization in the wrong direction; however, some of the tools presented here might help to avoid the most unfortunate situations. We recommend that project managers look closely to see if the goals – and the deliverables they imply – will contribute appropriately to the development of the organization. The mission breakdown structure, which we present later, is a very useful tool to analyse a project's alignment and what direction the project should take. Later we also introduce responsibility charts that are used to describe clearly the resource commitments of the base organization. Responsibility charts can reveal clearly the base organization's commitment to resources and what will happen if it doesn't provide them.

A project manager responsible for a project that lacks sufficient support is in a compromised position. Should he continue with the project? Or should he accept the inevitable and withdraw from further participation? The project manager is torn between loyalty for the task he has been given and consideration for his own career. Poor project results will usually reflect on the project manager, even if caused by factors beyond his control.

Stakeholders opposed

The creation of a project independent of the organization plans is the most dramatic pitfall because, more than anything else, it is the most likely to ensure the failure of the project. But there are other problems too. In today's complex world, a project affects a great many people. For example: a project may have consequences for employees, trade unions, creditors, customers, clients, suppliers and so on. If the project has some stakeholders with strong power or influence who are negative to the project or some aspects of it, they may have a devastating effect on the progress of the project.

A stakeholder analysis is useful for identifying the stakeholders and understanding their interests and possible contributions to the project. Inexperienced project planners often focus their planning effort on the system tasks of the project and may not pay attention to a well-thought-out handling of the stakeholders.

Undefined principles and policies of project work

Well-defined principles and policies for project work create the climate that ensures a project functions well. Sometimes these principles and policies are not agreed upon. Questions that should be answered in the general project guidelines include:

- What is the organization and line management's responsibility for the project work?
- Who is responsible for committing resources?
- What are the policies for making resources available?
- What are the tools and methods to be used for the management of the project?
- How are coordination and cooperation to be achieved?

If these general guidelines for project work are not defined in advance a project's momentum could be reduced. Valuable project time of the entire team is lost discussing principles that should have been clarified at the outset. A project is based on a certain understanding of the way people are to cooperate. If that understanding proves to be wrong, the project members will cease to work in harmony, and their efficiency will drop.

It is wise to state the principles and policies of project work before the project starts. In organizations that use projects extensively, one can often find project manuals or other written material stating the relationship between the project and the base organization.

The cracks in the foundation that we have discussed so far have focused on the interactions between the base organization and the project. We have pointed out problems that might arise. We have emphasized that project management cannot take on the responsibility for how the organization plans and prioritizes its development efforts. However, we have also given a strong warning, saying that the project manager has to make sure that the project has the backing of the base organization and its most important stakeholders. We have pointed out that it is of great importance for the project work to be in harmony with the organization work culture, and that the principles and policies of project work state this.

Imprecise goals

The floundering of many projects can be traced back to unclear or imprecise goals, with insufficient effort being put into defining the problems that the project should solve. It is an unfortunate human tendency to spend insufficient time on this and race on to design solutions before the problem is properly defined. When selecting a new IT system, it is easy for project members to enter quickly into discussions regarding technical matters before being clear on the changes the new system is meant to achieve. It is natural for technically oriented people to like concrete activities such as programming. Those activities are more engaging for them than abstract activities such as deciding what should be achieved.

We know that imprecise or even incorrect goals will have harmful effects on our projects and yet we are lured to the 'fast track'. How can we avoid this? We need methods and tools that 'force' project management to spend time on defining what the project shall achieve and therefore create a sound foundation for the project work.

Unbalanced levels of ambition

A PSO project results in different types of changes. With a focus on technical changes (a personal computer installed to access a new IT system), will users have the knowledge and skills to operate the equipment and the application software? And who is ensuring that organizational changes will clarify their new areas of responsibility? There is often a tendency in the specifications of projects to overemphasize the technical aspects and ignore the people and organizational aspects. We find it easier to imagine the concrete, technical tasks rather than the abstract, organizational and human ones.

Project managers must balance the PSO goals of projects. They must ensure that the technology introduced is the right response to the needs of the organization, and that the organization is left with the right people, with the right skills and adequate structures to use the technology. If the imbalance of these goals is apparent to the users they might resist the new system and cause the project to fail completely.

Project management must believe in the benefits of balanced PSO goals before it implements methods and tools that will help its project achieve appropriate balance.

PITFALLS IN PLANNING

Many factors can create pitfalls in planning. Figure 3.2 sums up the most dangerous.

- The planning level is uniform; the plan contains too much detail for some users, and too little for others
- The planning range is psychologically unsound
- The planning method discourages creativity, and encourages bureaucracy
- The planning estimates of time and cost are over-optimistic
- The planning of resources overestimates their competence and capacity
- Some factors are easily ignored by planners
- Lack of knowledge and understanding of the uncertainties involved

---

Figure 3.2 Pitfalls in planning

The planning level is uniform

The most serious pitfall in planning is to select one planning level that is uniform and consequently impractical. Making a plan at one level, we must either choose a plan that is too broad in scope, with insufficient detail for some of the people involved, or choose one that is too detailed, and hence does not present the overview of the project.

We need to view a plan at two levels at a minimum. One would be broad in scope and function as an overview plan that can be used in discussing the deliverables of the project. It can be used in the dialogue between the project owner and the project manager. It is not practical to use a detailed plan for reporting to senior managers. They are interested in whether or not the project will achieve its goals and they cannot see this in a mass of detailed activities. They need an overview such as a milestone plan that shows them whether or not the project is on target. If a milestone is missed, they may want additional information to show what corrective action should be taken. If the project is on target, they need only to be shown that it is.

On the other hand, the project staff cannot use a plan that is too broad in scope to coordinate their activities. If the tasks are too large, progress cannot be measured at regular intervals. There is a great chance of misunderstandings and the project members may do the work incorrectly or at an insufficient pace. Therefore, a more detailed view of the plan must exist to help coordinate the activities of the project members.

Project management requires at least two levels of planning, a milestone plan and an activity plan. The former level allows management to focus on 'what'; and the latter level allows team members to focus on 'how'.

The planning range is psychologically unsound

There is a tendency in many projects to focus on the overall final deadline. Too much attention is given to this date. By being concerned only about a point that lies far into the future the project members can feel that there is plenty of time to do the work. Consequently, the project may be viewed as a low priority and if Parkinson's Law holds, project members will fill the time with ineffective or inefficient work, or no work at all.

People tend to believe that any task may be postponed till the last possible finishing time. An analogy from school comes easy to mind. Most of us wrote our essay the day before it should be delivered, irrespective of the time we were given to do it. It is, in other words, unfortunate to have a planning horizon to far ahead – it is a pitfall. Project managers should set definitive short-term targets for the completion of work. We believe in the 'Monday principle'. Planning should give attention to what should be achieved before next Monday. To set short time horizons, the plan must contain goals and activities that are controllable in the short term, and towards which the project members can strive.

The planning method discourages creativity

At the opposite end of the spectrum from 'broad' plans are the unwieldy, overly detailed plans. Many of us have seen networks with thousands of activities. These plans hamper communication rather than enhance it.

Appropriate tools communicate the plan and report progress on single sheets of paper. A milestone plan and an associated definition of role responsibilities are on one sheet of paper each. Managers should not be burdened with comprehending reams of data in the short time they have available. The activities associated with each milestone are on one sheet of paper. Project members must be able to see their work easily and must not be burdened by having to trace a trail through a tortuous network with thousands of activities.

If the planning level, tools and range are cumbersome, then the project members will not engage in creative discussions about the plan. It is important that the language used in the plan be understandable to people, not just the specialist; it must be free of jargon.

Planning should be a group activity, where the relevant parties work together to solve the task at hand. It is in the execution of the task that people should take individual responsibility. However, it is common for the situation to be reversed. Inexperienced project managers plan the work in privacy, and then delegate the implementation to the group.

Over-optimism

Over-optimism might be due to genuine optimism or lack of realism, depending on your viewpoint. We have worked with companies with detailed methods for estimating the work content and cost of projects. These methods and empirical data are used to plan a project, but then they are overtaken by optimism. The managers look at the estimates, and think they are too high. They presume that it must be possible to do the work more quickly and cheaply. However, if you use estimating methods you must trust them and accept the results, otherwise the effort is wasted.

The other situation that can lead to this type of self-deception is when the project must be 'sold' to the base organization, or to an outside customer. To make the project attractive, the project manager reduces the estimates of work content and cost and then convinces himself that the new estimates can be achieved. Unfortunately, they usually cannot.

Another form of over-optimism is to underestimate the time required to achieve procedural changes. Empirical data exists to estimate the time required for technical activities. For example, we know how long it takes to pour 1,000 cubic metres of concrete for a factory foundation, and how long it takes to set. We know how long it takes an average programmer to write 1,000 lines of COBOL program.

In contrast, we do not know how long it takes to make a procedural change. We do not know how much resistance to the change there will be, and what mode of change can be adopted. Will it be short and sharp, or require months of persuasion? Further, if the progress of change is dependent on certain decisions being made within the organization, it is common to ignore the political factors underlying the decision, and to underestimate the time required.

The result is that insufficient time and resources are given for the procedural tasks. Time is not allowed for people to acquire new attitudes and new knowledge. Critical tasks are done inadequately and must be redone. Resources are wasted.

Over-optimism with projects is dangerous. To avoid this pitfall, those who will do the work must be involved in the planning; those who are responsible for the implementation must be realistic. It is important to consider the time and resources required to achieve a change; to unfreeze, to implement the change, and to refreeze the organization. These resources must be included in the plan.

Overestimating competence and capacity

This pitfall is related to the previous one and can contribute to it. Estimates of time and cost are often based on ideal resources, or ideal circumstances. However, the knowledge and experience of the staff available, and the time they can devote to the project, may be less than ideal. The important point is that plans must be formulated to take into account the actual constraints.

Further, users are often approached too late to provide resources for the project, or they are asked early enough but without obligation. Thus, when his input is required, the user has not made alternative arrangements, and the resources required are not available.

Factors ignored

There is a tendency to plan a project as if the outside world does not exist. However, people become ill, they go on holiday, and they attend courses and seminars. These factors reduce their capacity. Our experience is that the reduction can be as much as 20–30 per cent.

Furthermore, the plan may omit some activities. Because projects are unique, previous experience cannot prepare us for all the activities that may be involved. If we attempt to make a list of all the activities at the start of a project, like many people do when they plan at the detail level alone, something is bound to be forgotten. Checklists of activities from previous, similar projects help, but since no two projects are identical they must be used carefully. To overcome this pitfall we suggest a rolling wave approach to activity planning.

Uncertainties

Even if we plan as well as we can, uncertainties prevail. Plans are not reality. Events happen outside the control of the project and affect it. Even within the project we will not have full control; people are not machines, and performance varies. It is very important to get a picture of the uncertainties associated with the project and then decide how to deal with them.

PITFALLS IN ORGANIZING

We shall also discuss pitfalls in organizing. They are summed up in Figure 3.3.

* Alternative organizations for the project are not considered
* The distribution of responsibility is not defined and the principles of cooperation are unclear
* Key resources are not available when required
* Line managers are not committed and key resources are not motivated
* The project manager is a technocrat, rather than a manager, so he cannot delegate, coordinate and control

Figure 3.3 Pitfalls in organizing

Alternative organizations are not considered

When implementing an organization to manage a project, few stop to reflect upon alternative ways to organize. It has become so common to adopt a hierarchical structure, with steering committee (or management group), project manager, project groups and reference or consultative groups, that the possibility of other structures is ignored.

The organizational structure should be chosen to suit the particular project at hand. The traditional hierarchical structure, with a steering committee, project manager and project groups, is best suited to projects that imitate the base organization. Such projects are usually large, and have purely technical goals such as the construction of a bridge or a road. The people working on the project devote their entire time to it during their involvement. The final users of the product are not involved until during, or after, commissioning. The lines of communication and principles of cooperation are likely to have been well defined and tested during previous projects. This is often the case in contracting companies where project work is the usual role of the base organization.

This hierarchical organization structure is not the best alternative for PSO projects. In these types of projects, project members divide their time between project work and their normal duties in the base organization. For such situations we believe that the task-oriented matrix structure is preferable.

Responsibilities and principles of cooperation are not defined

The matrix organization requires that the lines of communication and the principles of cooperation be clarified. Decisions regarding how to resolve conflicts of priority between project work and the demands of the base organization are necessary. However, this is seldom done adequately and the project organization will not function properly.

Key resources are not available

The usual consequence of failing to clarify responsibilities and the principles of cooperation is that resources will be unavailable when required. Lack of the necessary resources will of course delay the project. The key resources are always people with specialist skills, and they are often the busiest people in an organization. Their line managers must agree to release them to the project at the right time. A well-functioning matrix organization is dependent on agreements between line managers and the project regarding when to release resources for project work.

Lack of motivation

The problem is aggravated if line managers do not arrange to cover the work of the key personnel assigned to work on projects. Those people must then do their normal work in addition to the project work. It is easy to understand why project members placed in this situation dislike project work, lose motivation, and inevitably delay the project. The result of accumulating delays will upset plans made by other managers releasing resources, and the project will enter a downward spiral.

A line manager's personal objectives can conflict with a project's goals. A project may be forced upon him from higher organizational levels, or he may not be familiar with development work. He may not have the energy or ability to attend to both project work and his daily routines. Faced with this situation, a line manager may sit on the fence, watching the project's progress. The consequence is that he will distance himself from decisions for which he has responsibility until it is too late.

Even if the project manager understands the line manager's lack of commitment to the project, he must not accept the situation and try to live with it, because a reluctant line manager can kill a project. The project manager must gain agreement with line managers regarding their responsibility to the project. If they cannot agree, negotiations must be escalated to higher levels in the base organization until the problem is resolved. But remember, if the line manager is to be committed, the problem must be resolved, not stamped on.

The project manager as leader

The last organizational pitfall is the selection of the wrong person as project manager. It is not uncommon to select a good technician, but such people are often not suitable.

Let's recall the important functions of a project manager: to plan, to organize and to control. A good technocrat will know the technical aspects of the work better than anyone else, but he may have problems delegating. He may believe, quite rightly, that he can do the work better and faster than his staff, and attempt to do so, with catastrophic results. He consequently neglects his managerial responsibilities as he works himself to death on the tasks he has assumed.

Who should be project manager – a technical expert, or a user? This question is irrelevant because the person should be chosen for his leadership qualities rather than his background. The project manager should be someone who:

- has the time and energy;
- can plan, organize and control the work methodically;
- can inspire others to work;

- can communicate in the best possible way with the base organization and the project participants.

PITFALLS IN CONTROLLING

Formulating a good plan is the first step in project management, and organizing the activities of project members is the second. However, project management is not about running ahead of the project members with the plan. It is about providing collaborative leadership from within the team. Control is an important part of that leadership.

Control is:

- reporting progress of the project in relation to the plan;
- analysing variance between progress and the plan;
- deciding which actions should be taken to eliminate variances;
- taking action.

Figure 3.4 presents what can create pitfalls in controlling.

- The project manager and his team do not understand the purpose of control; they do not understand the difference between monitoring and controlling
- The plan and progress reports are not integrated
- The project manager has responsibility, but no formal authority
- There is no well-defined, formalized communication between project manager and project members

---

Figure 3.4 Pitfalls in controlling

Misunderstanding the purpose of control

Many people do not understand the purpose of project control. The purpose is not to wield a stick, to apportion blame, or to punish the guilty. The purpose is to monitor progress, and to take corrective action in time.

We must stress the point that control is more than just monitoring and reporting progress. In many projects, control merely means writing a few familiar quotes to the project manager on the current status, or extending some lines on a bar chart to show how far the project has progressed. Perhaps the project manager reads what he gets and then conscientiously files the report, but that is where it usually ends. Reporting becomes a ritual you do because you are told to, rather than an activity you take seriously. Serious control means evaluating the consequences of deviations from the plan and acting upon them.

Poor integration between plans and progress reports

To facilitate control, the plan should encourage it. Therefore, we suggest that the reports should be written on the plan, so that it is reviewed whenever a report is made. This is not usually the case because plans are structured in such a way that control is an enormous administrative burden. They tend to be voluminous, but do not contain information that allows deviation to be analysed effectively.

The classic example is the large, multi-coloured network with thousands of activities that sometimes adorns a project manager's office. It does not encourage control because the effects of late activities on the project's duration are difficult to judge. It is impossible to monitor productivity from the productivity of individual activities. The assessment of quality is often left until the last activity is finished, and then it is too late.

The ideal plan invites control and provides information to the project manager enabling him to exercise it.

Responsibility without authority

The project manager will be unable to control if he does not have the same formal authority as the equivalent managers in the base organization from whom he is obtaining resources. If a project member has a conflict of priority between the project manager and his line manager, there is seldom any doubt where his loyalty lies. He will choose his line manager because the line manager pays his salary, and he must work for him when the project is finished.

The project manager is ultimately responsible for achieving the project's goals, and therefore must be given commensurate authority. A project manager with charisma will derive some authority from his personality, called personal power. However, average people will manage most projects, and what they lack in personal power they must be given in terms of positional power.

Their authority to control the project must be reflected in the project's organization.

No formalized communication

A mistake made by many project managers is not to review their staff's progress formally. For them, reviewing progress consists of striking up a conversation around the coffee machine. However, this kind of unsystematic, informal monitoring is inadequate, and is never taken seriously.

It is beneficial to have informal conversations on a project, because it aids creative communication, but for effective control, some communication must occur formally at regular intervals. Contact should occur at set times, with a predefined format. If not, staff lose respect for the review process and control will be ineffective.

PITFALLS IN EXECUTION OF PROJECT WORK

In the last four sections we described pitfalls that can arise in setting the management of a project: its foundation and subsequent planning, organizing and controlling. If these managerial details are wrong, professional technical competence is not enough to ensure success. Likewise, no amount of management aids can ensure success if professional technical competence is lacking. Both are crucial to success.

To end this discussion we consider some professional technical pitfalls that can arise in the project work. Many will be unique to a particular professional discipline. Figure 3.5 sums up what may create general pitfalls.

Problems of cooperation

One of the traits of a project already mentioned is that it requires a variety of resources. This can lead to a number of pitfalls in cooperation during implementation, especially the cooperation of unacquainted people.

Many people underestimate the difficulty of getting people to work together. This is further complicated if they have not

---

Problems of cooperation:
- The complexity of coordinating a variety of resources is underestimated
- The task of achieving cooperation between unacquainted people is not fully understood
- The technical methods are too complicated to be fully understood by the users
- Different people work by different rules and procedures

Problems of goal setting:
- Imprecise goals
- Changes to the plan or specification are uncontrolled

Problems of activity execution:
- Activities are not completed and documented before others begin
- Project members seek in vain the perfect solution
- Quality control is inadequate

Figure 3.5 Pitfalls in execution of project work

worked together before. In the extreme, no time or effort is put into creating cooperation, because the project manager does not believe it is important. This may be due to a lack of competence of the project manager, who may not know how to enhance cooperation or who may wrongly believe that the project members are used to working together.

It is normal for the future users to be represented on the project team. The different experience of the users and the experts can make cooperation difficult. The tools used by the experts can further complicate collaboration. Methods that describe the project's objectives in a way that is foreign to the future users, or use of jargon they cannot understand, hampers communication. The experts must describe the project in a language the users can understand, while retaining a degree of precision that describes succinctly the project's intent.

Project members may not all work by the same rules and procedures, or work may be documented in different ways. This weakens cooperation and reduces the potential for project members to benefit from each other's experience. It will also reduce the project manager's flexibility, as it will be hard to transfer people from one activity to another. Further, it is difficult to introduce new staff, as they must be trained in a variety of procedures. It is vital to define the principles of cooperation, and to establish a common set of rules and procedures to be used by people while working on the project.

Problems of goal setting

We discussed earlier the needs for precise and well-balanced goals. The scope of the project must also be defined. It is common that the project participants do not devote enough time to clarifying these matters.

Changes will inevitably occur during execution of a project, but uncontrolled changes can kill a project as the members are sucked into the spiral of planning and re-planning. Changes must be controlled and only included in the plan after they have been properly specified.

Problems of activity execution

If a project team consists of a fixed number of people, members may be under-utilized at times. To stop them from becoming dissatisfied, the project manager may try to keep them busy by starting work out of sequence before previous tasks are completed. If the results of the latter turn out to be other than expected, the former must be repeated. All work must be done in the correct order.

The technical work must not become the sole objective as it is done to meet project goals that usually also include targets for scope, time and cost. Experts often find it difficult to accept that they are not given enough time to find the perfect solution. There is a certain professional prestige in seeking an elegant solution. However, targets of time and cost are usually also important considerations requiring us to accept balanced solutions. The project manager must balance technical solutions and time and cost goals. This choice between must be negotiated with stakeholders.

The scenario above was between an imperfect, adequate solution, and targets of time and cost. To be able to judge whether the imperfect solution is adequate, the project manager must plan and control quality using milestones for control throughout the project. Leaving the assessment of quality until the end is dangerous, since it is then impossible to change it without incurring significant cost.

AVOIDING PITFALLS

We have considered a number of pitfalls that we know from experience can cause a project to fail. It is important to dispel any myth that there is some magic formula for estimating or planning a project that guarantees its success. Projects fail for far more fundamental reasons. The list may not be exhaustive, but they must all be avoided if the project is to have the greatest chance of success.

We have also suggested what can be done to avoid these pitfalls. These suggestions are summarized in Figure 3.6, which

- The project must work on tasks which are important to the base organization. There should be a close correlation between the direction of the company and the goals of the project
- The project must have an overview of all stakeholders and their expectations of the project
- The base organization should have principles and policies of project work
- Project methods and tools must compel those involved to spend time on defining project objectives and goals, ie what the project should achieve
- Project methods and tools must compel those involved to focus on giving the project a composite deliverable, which encompasses matters relating to people, systems (technical matters) and organization
- Project planning must take place at a minimum of two levels, the global (milestone) level and the detailed (activity) level
- Short-term, controllable intermediate goals must be set
- A plan must be clearly presented on one sheet of regularly sized paper
- Those who draw up the plans must know that they themselves will have to live with the consequences of them
- The project must have an overview of the uncertainties associated with the project and have decided how to relate to the uncertainties
- There must be an understanding of the fact that change processes take time
- There must be an understanding that a project can be organized in several different ways
- The lines of responsibility in the project must be clearly described
- Binding agreements for releasing resources for the project must be drawn up
- Line management and project members should be highly motivated
- A project manager with the right qualities must be selected
- There must be an understanding of what control is, and how important this task is in project work
- A plan must be formulated in such a way that it both facilitates and promotes control
- The project manager must be given authority in his dealing with the base organization
- Procedures for reporting must be established
- Concrete work must be done to create good conditions for cooperation in the project
- Common methods must be selected for work on the project which also encourage communication between the experts and users
- Changes in project objectives and goals must be made after careful consideration
- There must be quality control throughout the project

Figure 3.6 Important factors for avoiding pitfalls in projects

can be seen as a 'requirement specification' for good project management and good project management tools.

GDPM is a technique that provides methods and tools that help avoid pitfalls. In the following chapters, we describe how project management should be implemented. GDPM will then be measured against the requirement specifications at the end (Chapter 11).

4

Foundation of the project

In this chapter we will discuss what we call the foundation of the project. Figure 4.1 gives an overview of topics to be discussed.

The project owner in the base organization must decide what he wants from the project. He must express what the purpose of the project is: *Why* does the organization wish to undertake this project?

In general, the project should lay the foundation for a future desired situation for the organization. What this situation actually should look like depends fully on the organization and its preferences. It may, for example, wish to be more competitive in a certain marketplace, have a better functioning organization, or have more satisfied customers. The project owner should (preferably in a dialogue with the project manager) state the purpose of the project.

Furthermore, goals have to be set for the project. The goals should express that certain 'products' (deliverables) will be delivered within time and cost limits and with a certain quality. They should be stated in such a way that when they are achieved, they contribute to the purpose of the project. Project

---

- Deciding the purpose of the project: mission breakdown structure
- Understanding the interests of the stakeholders: stakeholder analysis
- Stating the foundation of the project: the project mandate
- Deciding the division of works and responsibilities between project and base organization: principle responsibility chart

Figure 4.1 The foundation of the project

deliverables bring the organization closer to the desired situation. There is a tight connection between the purpose and the goals of the project.

The mission breakdown structure is a tool that helps clarify the purpose of the project. It exhibits what the project might do for the organization.

Earlier, we pointed out the importance of having a project that is strongly supported by the base organization. It is of utmost importance to have the backing of the project owner, but there are many more entities to which the project should have close ties. It is essential for the project to have an understanding of all involved who have an interest in the project. We might get such an understanding through a stakeholder analysis. The results of the analysis may affect the goals of the project. By designing the project's deliverables with the stakeholders in mind, the satisfaction of some of them might improve.

The project mandate sums up the elements of the foundation of the project. It contains the main information about the basis for, and the direction of, the project. The project mandate is based on the insight gained from the mission breakdown structure and the stakeholder analysis.

The project will use resources from the base organization. The interplay between the base and the project is vital for project success. It is, as earlier stated, of importance to clarify in general the division of responsibilities between the project on one hand and the project owner and the base organization on the other. The principle responsibility chart is a helping tool in this illuminating process.

PURPOSE AND GOALS OF THE PROJECT

Initial project work starts by clarifying the purpose and goals of the project. They may be formulated by the project owner and be found in preliminary project documents, but there is always a need to elaborate on them and define them more precisely. We recommend that the project owner and the project manager do this as a joint effort. They may find it wise to include even more people.

A discussion of goals must take place at several levels. Figure 4.2 illustrates this.

When determining project goals with regard to PSO projects, you must anchor your discussions in the organization that the project is intended to change and improve. Every organization is established to fulfil a certain purpose. A college is set up to educate; a consulting firm offers advisory services; a factory manufactures and sells a certain product. In addition to carrying out the core tasks for which it is intended, an organization must have managing functions and administrative support functions (accounting, personnel administration and payroll departments, for example).

The legitimacy of the project lies in the fact that, in one way or another, it will enable the organization to achieve its main purposes better, or improve its performance of the managing or supporting functions. When public projects are concerned, it is often necessary to regard the whole of society as the receiving organization. The project should thus contribute to realizing a society's main purposes or needs.

A project cannot address every core, managing or supporting function in an organization; decisions must be made about which elements the project should promote. The purpose of the project is thus to contribute to the organization's ability to perform some of its tasks in new or improved ways.

A car importer wanted to develop a computer-based customer service system, a common project task. Before taking on the task, discussions were held about what the organization wished to achieve. What emerged from these discussions was that it wished to treat customers in a way that would encourage them

---

The company
- Core functions (the purpose of the company)
- Management functions
- Support functions

The purpose of the project

The goals of the project
- Main goals
- Subsidiary goals (the main goals divided into more detailed and measurable goals)

Figure 4.2 Different levels in the goal clarifying process

to remain customers for life. This insight led to an analysis of which aspects of car ownership and maintenance gave rise to brand loyalty and what that implied for service and quality standards in all branches of the organization. Only after completing this process was the purpose of the project clarified. The project thus went from the development of a simple computer system to a composite project where staff also worked to improve service and quality in all customer contact areas. The project had acquired a purpose ('Our customers remain loyal to the organization for life') that genuinely supported something of importance for the organization.

In another example, an organization determined that it wanted an improved financial management information system. However, again we emphasize that it is important to go beyond just the system requirements and consider the underlying organization's needs. In this case, the underlying need was to manage better the acquisition and utilization of resources, both people and equipment. Therefore, that was the true issue the project needed to address. For this purpose, a computer system was required to fulfil certain technical and functional requirements. Equally important, however, were organizational development and employee professional development that would lead to better usage of resources within the organization. The purpose of the project turned out to be: 'Competent and motivated finance professionals with the right tools'.

Product development is another common project task. The starting point must be to determine what the organization expects of a new product. It must satisfy certain customer needs and at the same time meet requirements, for example cost effectiveness and the ability to fit into the existing production and market profile. Even such an innovative project does not lead a life independent of the base organization. On the contrary, it must develop its ideas in harmony with the base organization and its needs. The purpose of the project may be 'The organization shall have a product that our customers demand, that fits into our product portfolio, and that we profit from.'

The project's purpose clarifies what the project will contribute to the organization. The goals of the project state concretely what it will deliver to the base organization.

Figure 4.3 illustrates the relation between the two concepts: purpose and goal. The project is a temporary organization that during its life brings into being several deliverables. The figure shows that the deliverables are conveyed gradually during the lifetime of the project (this is an evolutionary strategy, which is quite different from a revolutionary strategy where all the deliverables appear on the last day of the project). The deliverables with their costs, quality, and appearances in time determine to what extent the project has achieved its goals. The base organization must utilize the deliverables and determine the achievement of the purpose of the project.

A goal should be presented in such a way that one can easily answer Yes or No to the question: 'Has it been achieved?' If the goal for the project is to hand over a certain deliverable with specified quality at a certain time and within a certain cost limit, it is easy to check if the goal is achieved. We can respond with a Yes!

We often see goals being stated as an activity to be carried out. That is the wrong way to articulate a goal. It is the result of the activity that is of interest to the base organization, not the activity itself. It is of importance to distinguish between taking an educational course and having developed some specified skills. The goal should be some desired result (the skills), and not the activity (the course).

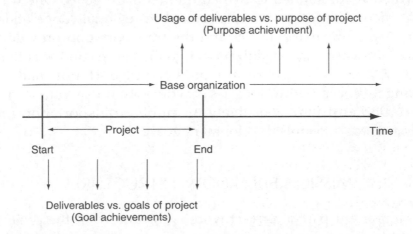

Figure 4.3 The purpose and goals of the project

The purpose expresses a future desired situation. The level of ambition may be high. We usually do not specify when it shall be reached. At a point in time, we do check to what extent (a certain degree) the purpose has been achieved (not a Yes or No answer).

The project goals form a hierarchy. Goals at lower levels are defined more precisely and elaborate the goals of the levels above. The need for the level of detail depends on the size of the project. The main goals of the project show the main areas to be addressed by the project. A thorough discussion of what the organization wants usually provides a good basis for establishing these goals. Usually there are several main goals (two to five).

In each case, a PSO test of the main goals should be carried out. This means that several goal-related questions should be answered. First, is there a goal for developing the people concerned? Second, is there a goal that states which 'technical items' will be produced by the project? Third, is there a goal for developing the organization?

A municipality proposed a project that would improve public transportation in the region. The project's purpose was 'Improve public transportation in region X.' Two main goals were formulated. One was that the trains should run more frequently. The second was that bus service should be expanded.

A PSO test of these main goals showed that they were purely 'technical'. Shouldn't the project also have 'P' and 'O' goals? Further discussion led to two additional main goals. One was that there should be an improvement in regional cooperation between municipal agencies and the transportation providers (in other words, an organizational goal). The second was that the citizens' attitude toward public transportation had to change. People had to look less favourably on private transportation and more positively on public transportation (in other words, a people development goal).

MISSION BREAKDOWN STRUCTURE

An important part of project work is to state what the project should achieve. The project owner should not be expected to do this by himself without proper help. The project team must also contribute, by clarifying the goals and anticipated results. This is not easy, especially when the project is extensive and complex, and the starting point is nothing more than a 'good idea'. The formulation of the goals often perpetuates the good intentions. There may be significant omissions of essential matters that have not yet been considered or discussed. Therefore it is useful to make a mission breakdown structure.

We distinguish, as stated above, between purpose and goals. Purpose has to do with meaningfulness and direction; while goals tell us what we shall specifically deliver. Thus it makes sense first to discuss the purpose of the project. We do that with the help of the tool we call the mission breakdown structure. In the following we will deal with:

- the purpose of a mission breakdown structure;
- the structure of the mission breakdown structure;
- the development of the mission breakdown structure.

Purpose of mission breakdown structure

We will use an example to illustrate this tool. Let us look at an organization that is considering the acquisition of a new computer-based accounting system. As we have learnt, it is wise to start by discussing why the organization should do this: what the purpose of the project is. The discussion reveals that the organization desires a situation where it has 'Good control of the organization's financial situation'.

It is useful to make a mission breakdown structure. The starting point will be the main purpose of the project. Thereafter we will break this main purpose into more detailed purposes that deepen it. Figure 4.4 shows what a very simple mission breakdown structure may look like.

The mission breakdown structure shows that achievement of the main purpose requires that employees be clever at financial control, that good software be available, and that clear lines of responsibility exist. We see the PSO thinking behind this: we need people with the right skills and attitudes (P), a computer-based system (S) and an organization with clarified responsibilities (O). Some of the purposes are broken down into more

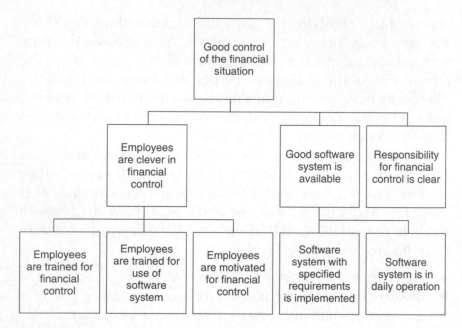

Figure 4.4 The mission breakdown structure of the project 'Implementation of new computer-based financial system'

detailed ones to illustrate the technique. In practical applications it is useful to do an extensive breakdown to familiarize oneself with the nature of the main purpose.

The mission breakdown structure will be used as the starting point for a discussion on the scope of the project; what shall be part of the project and what will be outside its responsibility. In the example the project takes on the implementation of the software and the training of the personnel in the use of the software. The rest of the work is left to the base organization. This is illustrated in Figure 4.5.

This precise identification of the area for project work is important. When a project is established, most people within the base organization believe that all development tasks belong to the project. At the same time, the project expects the base organization to take care of many of those same tasks. The clarifying process through the mission breakdown structure is important to create a sound basis for the project.

We see that it is not necessarily for the project to have responsibility for everything covered by the purpose of the project. It is

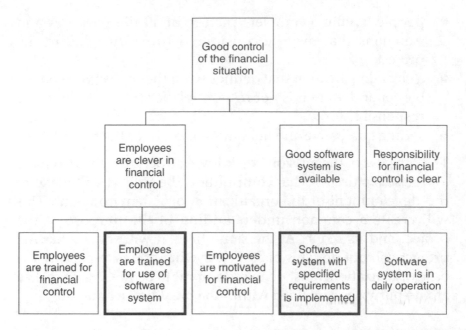

Figure 4.5 The mission breakdown structure of the project 'Implementation of new computer-based financial system' with project scope marked

quite natural that some operational tasks (like the running of the computers and its application software) should be the base organization's responsibility (for example, IT operations). It is also possible to allocate certain development tasks to the base such as the task of motivating employees to exert sound financial control. PSO projects do not necessarily have the responsibility for all elements of P, S and O.

The mission breakdown structure could further be used to state the particular results one would like to achieve for the specified purposes. We use the breakdown structure as a vehicle for setting the main goals of the project. The example shows that the project has responsibility for training people in the use of the software. The goal should express what the project should deliver such as a specific number of trained people with specified skills.

Work on the mission breakdown structure should result in:

- everyone involved having a common understanding of what the project purpose is;

- people having a complete picture of all the purposes and functions that may be considered to be included in the project;
- a clear demarcation that defines what the project is responsible for and what it is not responsible for (ie what others are responsible for);
- setting qualitative and quantitative goals for the project.

The purpose of the mission breakdown structure is thus to create a precise picture of what contribution the project will make to the development of the organization or its environment. This will create a common understanding of the purpose of the project and its scope. At the same time, it will show what the project will not do. This makes clear what others, especially the base organization, must do in order for it to be possible to realize all the purposes contained within the breakdown structure.

Structure of mission breakdown structure

We will start with the heading. It expresses the main purpose upon which the whole mission breakdown structure is to be built. The main purpose can be divided into a maximum of seven purposes. More than seven would probably not represent a balanced picture. Some of them would most likely be more important than others and it would present a weaker overview.

The contents of the mission breakdown structure cannot be standardized. Each case must be discussed on its own merits. We recommend using the PSO thinking. But there is no reason to be a fanatic; other groupings can be more enlightening and a better basis for division of responsibilities. It may be wise to think of vital stakeholders and their interests (we discuss the importance of identifying the stakeholders and their wishes below).

Sometimes it is wise to include in the mission breakdown structure necessary supplementary functions to be carried out to achieve the situation described by the main purpose. These could be management functions (leadership in general or within certain areas, or basic prerequisites for obtaining the main purpose) and supportive or administrative functions (IT, personnel, accounting, operations). We usually place the core purposes in the middle of the structure, with the management functions on the right and supporting functions on the left.

It is important to expend sufficient effort to develop an effective structure. There should be little grey area between the columns. If you continue to have problems placing items, the headings should be moved or adjusted.

The wording of the purposes is important and worth formulating carefully. It is often difficult to formulate the main purpose, the basic idea, and it is easy to create descriptions that are lengthy, but unhelpful. The mission breakdown structure is a means of communication. Therefore, it should communicate accurately.

It is important to bear in mind that the mission breakdown structure is quite different from the work breakdown structure (WBS) found in many other project management toolboxes. The mission breakdown structure expresses desired situations; it does not identify activities as in a WBS. At a much later stage we will determine which activities are to be carried out. Even when the mission breakdown structure includes management and support functions, they should be described as requirements or desired situations, not as activities to be carried out.

It is sometimes necessary to supplement the mission breakdown structure with a document with more detailed descriptions. The following topics may be covered:

- Explanation: For each box we can explain the content in more detail.
- Clarifying responsibility: Responsibilities for the different purposes may be expressed.
- Importance and cover: The importance of each purpose may be stated along with an explanation as to how well it is achieved today.
- Solution: Goals and ways of achieving the purpose may be stated.

Development of mission breakdown structure

The method or approach for developing the mission breakdown structure is similar to the one we will recommend later on for developing milestone plans. It is essentially a group task, but the group must not be too large. Eight people are probably the upper limit. The group leader needs to organize the process in advance but other participants need only come fresh and free from other demands on their time.

The group room should be equipped with a whiteboard and a flip chart. A full day should normally be set aside. It may be appropriate to present a preliminary structure back to others in the base organization for comment and then resume work, say, a week later.

The process itself is simple:

- Begin with the main purpose and discuss sub-elements.
- Try different formulations. When the group has agreed on a usable starting point, write the formulation with a non-permanent pen on the board.
- Enter keywords in the structure and headings for the lower levels.
- Write up proposed texts for these.
- Adjust the main purpose if necessary.
- Continue column by column to find a structure for the lower levels.
- Write up the text.

We use a whiteboard, which enables us to make changes easily. It is also a work form that facilitates effective group work. It may take from one to three days, depending on complexity, to develop a mission breakdown structure that will adequately support further planning.

STAKEHOLDERS AND STAKEHOLDER ANALYSIS

Stakeholders are individuals and groups who are actively involved in the project. Stakeholders are also those who are positively and negatively affected by project work or deliverables from the project. The first-mentioned category of stakeholders are called internal, the rest are external. When we include the external stakeholders, the project will have a considerable number of stakeholders. Most of them are probably in favour of the project, but some may be opposed to it.

It is important to identify the stakeholders, for several reasons. We do a stakeholder analysis to help the project:

- familiarize itself with the stakeholders;
- understand how the coalition of stakeholders can be kept together;
- balance the contributions of the stakeholders and the rewards they will receive from the project;
- establish information distribution;
- establish a basis for goal setting.

It is helpful for the project manager to regard the project as a coalition of stakeholders, which means a network of individuals and groups who have the intention of creating something together. This network or alliance is not of a contractual type, but purely mental. If the project manager views the project as a network of stakeholders, he will try to keep it together to achieve the best possible results. The project will need the common efforts of the stakeholders. But the project manager may be faced with situations where some may withhold contributions because they feel that what they do for the project is not in balance with what they will get in return. The project manager must seek to retain the balance between the contributions and the rewards.

During the stakeholder analysis we identify the stakeholders and describe their relationships to the project, especially their areas of interest, the kinds of contributions the project needs from them, and what they expect in return from the project. We also look at what kind of power the stakeholders possess and what they may do if they disagree with project results or processes.

Figure 4.6 shows how we may present the results from the stakeholder analysis as a table. It covers the most important factors, like:

- the area of interest of the stakeholder (for instance, special deliverables or special tasks of the project);
- the contributions of the stakeholder (for instance, resources like work or financial capital or other types of positive or negative engagements);
- the expectations of the stakeholder (what the stakeholder expects from the project, which might be deliverables or jobs; what we call the rewards from the project);

- the power of the stakeholder (the way the stakeholder can affect the project in case of a conflict and whether it can increase its power by cooperating with others);
- the appropriate strategy to work with the stakeholder (the way the stakeholder should be treated by the project);
- person responsible for implementing the strategy (the person within the project who is responsible to carry out the strategy).

Stakeholder	Area of interest	Contri-butions	Expecta-tions	Power	Strategy	Respon-sible

Figure 4.6 Table for stakeholder analysis

A project has multiple stakeholders. Figure 4.7 names some of the most common. Such a list is a useful reference when the project needs to identify its own stakeholders.

- Shareholders
- Top management
- Line managers
- Users
- Cooperating partners
- Competitors
- Creditors (banks)
- Suppliers
- Customers
- Customer organization
- Government
- Public officials
- Political parties
- Politicians
- Interest groups
- Individuals
- Labour unions
- Members of local labour unions
- Media
- Researchers
- Religious organizations

Figure 4.7 Common stakeholders

The stakeholder analysis should be carried out early in the project – it is part of creating the foundation for the project. The results can be used to evaluate the main goals of the project and see how they fulfil the expectations of the different stakeholders. The goals may be changed somewhat to increase the support for the project. The stakeholder analysis is also of value when determining how to inform the stakeholders of the progress of the project.

PROJECT MANDATE

In order to make a decision as to whether a project should be started or not, the project owner needs a description of the important aspects of the project. Various terms are in common use for this, such as project statement, project directive, project outline, etc, but we use the term project mandate. Figure 4.8 shows what such a description should include. The project mandate sums up the foundations of the project. The purpose and goals of the project are the main ingredients of the mandate.

We discuss these elements in more detail below.

Creating the mandate

The project mandate must evolve through analysis and discussion. It is not possible to formulate a good and well-thought-out project mandate without carrying out basic groundwork. Many project mandates are established without the necessary thorough consideration. Therefore, they must not be regarded as 'sacred cows' that cannot be changed. Through discussions within the project and with the project owner the project is described and defined more precisely; it may be expanded, narrowed down, or in certain cases, divided up into several projects.

- Name of the project
- Project owner
- Project background
- Purpose of the project
- Goals of the project
- Project scope (included and excluded)
- Limitations on project work
- Project budget

Figure 4.8 The project mandate

An oil organization in the North Sea initiated a project to develop an inspection system for their platforms and pipelines. When the project began to discuss the inspection system, it was quickly discovered that there was a major difference between inspection of the platforms (technical inspection with trained personnel) and inspection of the pipelines (which was to be performed by unmanned submarines). There was no particular purpose to be served in developing one common inspection system. As a consequence, there was no reason for establishing one project covering both aspects even though it was in the project mandate. The story illustrates that project managers should not accept mandates without first analysing whether they are properly defined.

Project name

Choosing the right name for a project is important. It might seem strange for this to be significant, but a name sends strong signals about what a project is about. The attitude of both the line management and the project team is affected by the name. Whether we like it or not, a project's name says something about the project. It is important that the project's name provides all the right associations and an understanding of what the project is aiming to achieve.

It is often appropriate that the purpose of the project be reflected in its name. The purpose expresses what the project should achieve, but the name should perhaps in a few words present a 'sales pitch' so that people immediately have a picture of what the project is aiming at. If a phase (sub-project) in a larger project is given its own name, the name should reflect the purpose of that part of the project.

Some examples illustrate the importance of a good project name. A project in an insurance organization was first described as 'Finance Section Reorganization'. It was decided instead to call it 'Reorganizing the finance section for better customer service'. The first name is associated with pure reorganization, to which many will immediately have a negative reaction. The second clarifies the purpose of the reorganization and creates motivation for the project.

A retail chain established a project to develop a lighting system for its stores. The project was to find and purchase the light fittings. The first proposal for a name, naturally enough, was 'Store Lighting System'. It would have been easy to believe that this was a purely technical project. A name which better illustrated what was to be achieved, however, was 'Sales Promoting Lighting'. Thus everyone involved understood that this was a project that also affected the stores' income. Interest in the project and commitment to it then changed significantly.

The development of a departmental report to be presented to Parliament can be regarded as a project, which involves many people, both inside and outside the department. One such project was first labelled 'Development of a departmental report on the reorganization of the central administration of education'. This designation gave the impression of a purely specialist task; some departmental bureaucrats were to write a report for Parliament. The name was changed to 'Political support for a departmental report on…'. The task was no different from the previous one; all departmental reports must have political support. This new name, however, painted a clearer picture of the project. Everyone understood that a report was to be written, but now the name highlighted the fact that this report must have support among the department's political leaders as well as of other politicians. It called attention to the fact that political aspects must be worked on in parallel with the formulation of the contents of the report.

The project 'To establish the State Film Institute' was renamed 'To establish and develop the State Film Institute for effective encouragement and promulgation of Norwegian films and film culture'. The name then illustrated the purpose of establishing the new institute.

Project names have had a tendency to be a bit long and detailed. A short, explicit name is better than a long one but sometimes it is necessary to use a longer name to get the meaning right. Many projects also acquire so-called acronyms, a word formed from the first letters of a complete name. PSO is an acronym for people, system and organization development. It is by far the best when an acronym for a project expresses the same concept as is contained in the complete project name, or the project's purpose.

Project owner

It is important to emphasize who has the main responsibility for the project on behalf of the base organization. We call the person the project owner. Project sponsor is also commonly used as a reference to this position. We like the term project owner; it symbolizes that the person has an ownership relationship to the project and in that sense a considerable responsibility.

A project creates a basis for changes and it will always be difficult to implement changes. A positive transformation process is only possible with strong support from people of the base organization. Carrying the title of project owner reminds the person to take his role very seriously.

The division of work and responsibilities between the project owner and the project has to be agreed on. We present the principle responsibility chart below. It is used to clarify these matters.

Project background

A project does not arise from nothing. It has a prehistory. In order to understand the reasons for the project it is useful to know its background. Then it is easier to know why it was started and understand its mission or purpose.

In this part of the mandate we describe earlier projects or activities of the base organization of relevance to the project. The relations to other ongoing projects should be mentioned.

The stakeholder analysis showed how stakeholders relate to the project. Such information may also give a better understanding of the background of the project.

Purpose and goals of project

The mandate presents the purpose and goals of the project. The goals may change during the project. The purpose, however, will stay unchanged during the whole project.

As we work on the project we gain further insight and knowledge. This gives us reasons to re-evaluate the aptness of the goals. Would other results or other deliverables than the ones we have planned for be more appropriate in order to achieve the purpose of the project? This is a justifiable question. The goals should not be considered untouchable. The most important thing is that the project contributes to the desired development of the base organization. To obtain the best results, we might find it necessary to change direction and set new goals.

In addition, changes in the environment of the project or base organization may also 'force' us to re-evaluate the goals. It is meaningless to pursue goals that no longer will give the desired result. Instead, we should, as a consequence of changes in the environment, change the planned deliverables and set new goals, which will benefit the base organization.

It is the duty of the project manager to assess whether existing goals are the most appropriate ones. This is a difficult task for him and he may be in two minds in this matter. He might feel that he was given a specified task with defined goals and that he is doing his utmost to succeed. At the same time it is his obligation to review whether the goals are right; this may cause frustration. The message here is that the most important thing for the project is to generate the best possible deliverables for the base organization and not what was considered to be the best when the mandate was created.

The purpose will stay unchanged. It is difficult to imagine a situation where the purpose of the project loses its relevance. If so, the project should be cancelled.

Project scope (included and excluded)

As pointed out above, it is important to clarify what the responsibilities of the project are and what it shall not be concerned with. The mission breakdown structure was made in order to discuss such matters. The decisions made may be marked on the structure itself. The mandate should refer to this document.

The project scope will state what the project bears responsibilities for, that is, what is included in the scope of the project and what is excluded from it.

Limitations to project work

The mandate should point out which limitations are placed on the project work. The limitations reduce the project's freedom to act. The limitations could be of quite a different nature, such as:

- restrictions on acquiring new equipment or material;
- limits on time available;
- cost limits;
- unacceptable actions (what the project is not allowed to do);
- unacceptable solutions (what the project is not allowed to study or suggest).

For example, the mandate can instruct the project not to buy new equipment such as new computers for its staff. Or if it is allowed, the mandate can instruct the project to buy new equipment through the purchasing department of the organization according to the rules of the organization. The limitations may also state that there are restrictions on time and costs available for the project. There might be further restrictions on what the project is allowed to do, for instance restrictions on foreign travel or hiring of external consultants. Restrictions on acceptable solutions might be stated such that the project cannot propose solutions that introduce layoffs, or move the organization abroad. These types of restrictions will reduce situations to which the project owner will react negatively.

Project budget

The mandate might include a presentation of the economic matters of the project. More specific and detailed documents may supplement the mandate on this subject. A thorough discussion of the economics of the project may need more space than is available on the mandate. As a minimum the mandate must present the costs of the project.

It is also beneficial to state the expected profitability of the project. That is, of course, more difficult than just the description of costs, but at least the project should be able to indicate the size of the profitability. There might be several reasons for starting a project, and profit may not be the only one, but no organization can survive in the long run if it has only unprofitable projects, so it is nice to know the fruitfulness of the project.

To calculate the profit of the project, we need to know the income or benefit. Profit is, of course, the difference between income and costs. The problem for a project is that the income will appear after the end of project. Moreover, it is the base organization and its people who will have the responsibility for creating the income or the benefits of the project. They will do that on the basis of what the project has delivered. Some of these income elements are difficult to quantify since they are of a 'soft' nature like better working environment or better reputation in the marketplace. It is easier to quantify the effects if the project contributes to increased sales.

The presentation of the profitability of the project has a wider purpose than just showing its profits calculated as net present value or other profitability concepts. It will also focus on who is responsible for creating the profitability. Of course, it is basically the responsibility of the project owner, but he has to rely on the members of the base organization. It will probably be very difficult to have the income (both the quantitative and the qualitative elements) and profitability generated if the responsibilities for achieving them are not clarified. It is further an advantage that the people responsible know the size of their obligations.

DIVISION OF RESPONSIBILITY BETWEEN BASE AND PROJECT: THE PRINCIPLE RESPONSIBILITY CHART

We have emphasized several times the importance of clarifying and illuminating the division of responsibilities between the base organization and the project owner on one hand and the project manager and project participants on the other. If an organization has several projects, it is wise to elaborate the principles for dividing responsibilities between these parties so they are the same for all projects. These principles could then be agreed on once and made valid for all project work within the organization. They become part of the foundation of all projects.

The principles can be presented verbally (as plain text), but we choose to present them as a table, which we call a principle responsibility chart. It gives a more concise view of the responsibilities of those involved. (We will later discuss the use of responsible charts in general.) On the principle responsibility chart the responsibilities for general project organizational and administrative matters are clarified, as well as professional matters of principle.

A principle responsibility chart, which encompasses all projects, is of great importance for the organization's project culture and project efficiency. It does away with the need for every individual project to discuss general project organizational and administrative matters. One can simply refer to the principle responsibility chart for projects.

Figure 4.9 shows an example of a principle responsibility chart. It illustrates matters that may be desirable to clarify using this type of

	Managing director	Project owner	Affected line manager	Affected base member	Project manager	Imple- menter	Elected represen- tative
Principle responsibility chart	D	C	C	I	X/P		C
Milestone plan and project responsibility chart	I	D	X	X	X/P	X	I
Allocation of resources, global level	D	d	X	I	P	C	I
Milestone report		D	C	I	X/P	C	I
Activity plan- ning		C	C		X/P	C	
– select imple- menter				d	d/P	C	
– determine duration of activity					X/P	X	
– determine start time and sequence					D		
– commit resources			d			d	
– release base resources			X/P			X	
– execute activity				C	P	X	
Activity report					X/P	C	

Figure 4.9 Example of principle responsibility chart

IX Executes the work
D Takes decision solely or ultimately
d Takes decision jointly or partly
C Must be consulted
I Must be informed
P Manages work and controls progress

responsibility chart. In the example, the roles the different parties have are also stated. We stress that what is stated in the figure is only an example and is not universally valid. Indeed, the discussion leading to the responsibility chart involves precisely the taking of decisions on the role of the different parties in the project.

In the example the following managerial functions are represented:

- managing director (the top executive manager of the organization);
- project owner (the one in the base organization who has the main responsibility for the project);
- affected line manager (those line managers who supply resources to the project or in other ways are affected by it);
- affected base member (those members of the base organization who are future users of the deliverables of the project or are in other ways affected by it);
- project manager;
- implementer (those project participants who carry out the actual activity);
- elected representative (the representative from the local labour union).

The first four instances belong to the base organization; the two next are part of the project organization. We have also indicated that an elected representative of the local labour union may be part of the project work.

The principle responsibility chart shows who has the responsibility for the different tasks. The example is based on the assumption that the implementers of the project (those who do project work) have a daily job in the base organization and must divide their time between that work and the project work. For this situation to function effectively, it is necessary to have clear lines of responsibility. The principle responsibility chart of Figure 4.9 shows an appropriate division of responsibilities and work when the project is an integrated part of the base organization.

The principle responsibility chart shows who is responsible for the chart itself. The example illustrates that we feel it is appropriate for the managing director to approve it. The top manager should approve the principles on which project work will be run in the organization.

The principle responsibility chart also establishes who plays a role in drawing up the global plan of the project (the milestone plan) and executing the plan (the milestone responsibility chart). An important aspect of planning and organization at this level is to get resources allocated to the project. The principle responsibility chart also shows who is responsible for this. The milestone report provides a report on the progress of the project.

The principle responsibility chart shows how detailed planning can be done. It is first looked at in a general way; it is ascertained that it is the project manager's responsibility. The project manager must lead and take responsibility for activity planning. At the same time it is made clear that the line manager and those carrying out tasks must be consulted on all essential matters. These are thus the leading roles in the detailed planning work.

A further, more precise definition is given to certain important tasks. It is the project manager and the line manager who will agree jointly on who from the base organization should perform tasks for the project. The personnel proposed must have an opportunity to give their opinion on the matter before the decision is made.

When planning project work, the resources needed for the individual activities to be executed must be evaluated. The project manager and those who will perform the activities should do this jointly. They should determine together how demanding on resources an activity is.

If the project manager makes the evaluation alone, it will not be binding on those who will perform the job. Unfortunately, some project managers behave somewhat tyrannically. First they commit themselves externally concerning how long an activity will take, and then they compel the implementer to accept the commitment. This can work, but it usually does not. The implementer is in a difficult position regardless of what the result is. If he does not manage to meet deadlines, he will be criticized unfairly. If he does meet them, he will be given new tasks with the same pressure. Neither is it correct for the implementer alone to evaluate how much work an activity demands. The project manager must be included, because he has experience and because he needs the insight provided by a thorough discussion of the requirements of an activity. Some implementers are over-optimistic; then the project manager must make adjustments.

Some project managers have acquired the habit of consistently lowering the estimates of the implementer. This is a dangerous policy. In the course of time the result will be that the implementer will not feel bound by these estimates; they are looked upon as the sole responsibility of the project manager. The ideal situation is that a good relationship based on openness and trust between the project manager and the implementer allows them to arrive at a mutual agreement on the extent of resources required to carry out the activities.

It is the project manager's responsibility, based on an assessment of the dependencies between activities in the project, to determine when an activity should be performed. The line managers and the implementers must together commit themselves to making resources available at the right time. The commitment must be mutual; neither the line manager nor the implementer can make commitments by themselves. If only one of them makes the decision, it may clash with the other's arrangements. The result will be that the resources are not available for the project when they are needed.

Those who have the executing responsibility will carry out the project activities. The line manager's responsibility, however, is to see to it that the implementers are released from their line duties so they can do project tasks. The line manager must plan his use of resources in the base organization so that he can make them available to the project when agreed. His plan must state which members of the base organization will take over assignments from those taking on project tasks. While doing the planning, the line manager must consult with the implementer's supervisor.

The responsibility for allocating resources to the project can be made perfectly clear, and straightforward agreements may be reached. Nevertheless, it is sometimes difficult to implement these agreements in practice. A generally positive climate must be created for the use of resources for development work. All the plans and agreements in the world will be of no use if the people in the base organization do not support them.

Situations may arise that make it necessary to re-evaluate the project plan and the allocation of resources for the project. The project plan is not a 'sacred cow' that cannot be touched. Conditions may arise that are so important that changes to the plan must be accepted.

Let us say that a computer-based invoicing system is to be installed in an organization. There are two people in the accounting department, and it is agreed that one of them should be released part-time to participate in developing the new invoicing system. But then the other person falls ill. There is then a choice between keeping to the project plan and stopping organization invoicing for a time, or continuing to invoice and letting the project plan fall apart. In such situations it is obvious that priorities and plans for the project must be reassessed.

Changes to the plan must thus be accepted. The important point is that a system is in place, which can discover at an early stage that the plans are not being adhered to. Then there is a chance to introduce measures to set a new course. We will discuss this in more detail in the chapter on control. The principle responsibility chart states that it is the implementers' responsibility to prepare the activity reports on project progress. They provide the project manager with the basis for preparing the milestone reports that show where the project is in relation to the project milestones.

On the principle responsibility chart we can also show who is responsible for making decisions on professionally related matters that may arise in the project. The general principle is that decisions should be made by whoever is responsible for these fields in the base organization. However, it may sometimes be useful to define precisely how professional questions should be handled.

SMALL EXAMPLE: PROJECT 'EXCELLENT PHYSICAL WORK ENVIRONMENT'

We shall present a simple example. We have reduced the realism a bit to emphasize the method. (A more extensive example is presented in Chapter 11.) The starting point is an organization that is dissatisfied with its work environment. The managing director wants to correct this. He sets up a project.

In order to formulate the project, he finds it useful to make a mission breakdown structure. Firstly, the main purpose of the project has to be stated. Thereafter, the purpose is divided into more detailed purposes, each of them contributing to the achievement of the main purpose.

In this case the purpose would be to have an organization that is functioning well and has an excellent work environment. Figure 4.10 shows the mission breakdown structure. An excellent physical work environment, an excellent social work environment, and a salary system with bonuses and incentives can achieve an excellent work environment. Further breakdown can be done, but is not shown here.

The mission breakdown structure serves as the basis for a discussion of what the project should take on and what should be outside the responsibility of the project. In this case the project owner (the managing director) decides to delimit the project to the physical work environment. He postpones work on the social work environment, which he finds much more difficult. He leaves the work of improving the salary system to the joint effort of the personnel division and the local labour union.

The purpose of the project is still to contribute to an excellent work environment, but the scope of the project is limited to the physical work environment.

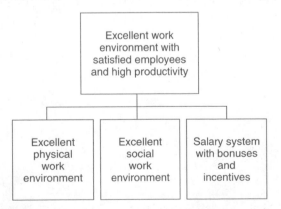

Figure 4.10 Mission breakdown structure for a project to create an excellent work environment

The project owner has chosen a relative low level of ambition for the project. The goal is to present an action plan to the managing director for an excellent physical work environment. The project is like a feasibility study. It is not given the responsibility for actually implementing the action plan.

A stakeholder analysis (Figure 4.11) has been conducted to identify the different individuals and groups who have an interest in the project. The stakeholders primarily come from the base organization, but we have included one external stakeholder, namely the potential suppliers of services in connection with the refurbishing of the premises of the organization.

It is an important part of the stakeholder analysis to decide which strategy to apply to each stakeholder and who should be responsible for its implementation. In the example the project manager is given responsibility for all stakeholder strategy implementation; this might not be the case in a larger project.

Based on the mission breakdown structure, the stakeholder analysis, and general discussions, the project mandate is set up. It is shown as Figure 4.12 on page 66. The project is named 'Excellent physical work environment'.

Stakeholder	Area of interest	Contribution	Expectations	Power	Strategy	Responsible
Managing director	Project's results and process	Support to project	High productivity Satisfied employees	Can stop project	Keep him happy	Project manager
Line managers	Project's results and process	Problem clarification Ideas for improvement	Better functioning organization Afraid of increased costs	Can refuse to support project	Involve them in project	Project manager
Employees of base organization	Project's results and process	Problem clarification Ideas for improvement	Better work environment	Can refuse to support project	Involve them in project	Project manager
Elected representative	Project's results and process	Support to project	Formal role in project Allowed to come forward with views	Can obstruct project's progress	Involve elected representative in project	Project manager
Potential suppliers	Orders when refurbishing	Ideas Offers with cost estimates	Sales	Can refuse to support project	Inform	Project manager

Figure 4.11 Stakeholder analysis for a project to create an excellent work environment

---

Project mandate

Name of the project
Excellent physical work environment

Project owner
Managing director

Project background
Poor physical work environment, hampering motivation and productivity

Purpose of the project
Excellent work environment

Goals of the project
Action plan for better physical work environment submitted to the managing director

Project scope (included and excluded)
See the mission breakdown structure of the project:
• Excellent physical work environment (included)
• Excellent social work environment (excluded)
• Salary system with bonuses and incentives (excluded)

Limitations on project
• Should not acquire new premises
• Should not propose changes that may cost more than USD 200,000
• Should be finished within half a year
• Employees and elected representative should be involved in project
  (see stakeholder analysis)

Project budget
Cost limit is USD 30,000, plus the time employees spend on project

---

Figure 4.12 Mandate for the project 'Excellent physical work environment'

5

Global planning – milestone planning

The discussion in Chapter 3 on pitfalls illustrated the importance of planning a project. Without planning you may stumble
into one or more of the pitfalls outlined there. The purpose of
planning is shown in Figure 5.1. Planning is both process
oriented (we get a mutual learning experience and create
common understanding) and product oriented (we produce
the plan, that is, the base for execution and control). The two
first-mentioned purposes belong to the process part, the others
to the product.

We differentiate between milestone planning and detailed
planning (which we also call activity planning). This chapter
covers milestone planning, but before we deal with this we will
look at some general principles of project planning. We will also
discuss whether the plan should be segmented into several
plans.

- To achieve a common understanding of the task to be resolved
- To obtain an overview of the work to be carried out
- To lay the foundation for allocating and committing resources
- To lay the foundation for a suitable organization of work
- To lay the foundation for monitoring and control

Figure 5.1 The purpose of planning

PRINCIPLES OF PROJECT PLANNING

Motivational planning

Planning should provide everyone involved in the project with a common understanding of the project. Planning should motivate project members for the task and provide them with a platform for cooperation. The process should stimulate the involvement of interested parties in the planning stages as well as in the subsequent implementation of the plans.

We shall go so far as to say that planning should be fun. Planning should be an opportunity to think anew and form different perspectives and to test ideas in a stimulating environment. We strongly emphasize the motivational and inspirational aspects of planning. They are often neglected in practice so that planning becomes a tedious chore carried out on the project manager's desk or PC. This results in a lack of ownership of the plan by the parties involved in the project and consequently the plan is never actively used. This is one reason for the failure of so many projects.

Planning must be a group activity. If all the central project members are involved, they acquire a common insight into the project and a common understanding of future requirements. Our experience is that 80–90 per cent of the time consumed in planning meetings of this kind is devoted to discussions around project content and problem solving. Only 10–20 per cent is formal planning.

Levels of planning

We divide planning into two fundamentally different levels. This is essential to draw up plans that will be effective in implementation and monitoring as well as getting the involvement of the personnel concerned. There must be one level where decisions are made upon what results the project is to deliver, and one level that describes how the results are to be achieved. It should be obvious that concentrating on planning *what* should be accomplished before discussing *how* is extremely important. This is called layered planning.

The division into what-planning (goal directed planning) and how-planning (activity planning) does not apply only to the planning of projects. This principle can also be applied to other areas. In marketing, for example, it is natural to discuss what is to be achieved before planning which media should be used and how the advertising campaign should be designed. When designing a computer system, it is necessary to discuss what the computer system should do for the users before discussing how to address those needs.

Planning at these two levels is a prerequisite for success because it means that planners and all those involved in the project are forced to discuss the challenges of the project in a logical order. Further, it makes it possible for those interested in the project to become involved in discussions and to obtain information at the level their needs and fields of knowledge dictate. This differentiation of planning levels makes it easier for different categories of interested parties to contribute to the process.

One consequence of a plan should be that interested parties commit themselves to it. Solid commitment is impossible without a good understanding of what the plan involves. It is impossible for various parties to become involved in a plan and to commit to it if the plan does not concentrate on their specific concerns and areas of responsibility. Therefore, planning in stages is also a prerequisite for establishing commitment in project work.

The most common mistake is to concentrate planning at the level of detailed specifications crammed with special terminology. Plans at that level do not provide an overview, nor do they encourage discussions about the main thrust of the project as they only present details. This frustrates line management and non-specialists. They may feel an inability to contribute and lose interest in the project. Who can blame them if they disclaim responsibility for project results.

Such planning makes it impossible to follow up in a meaningful way. Control, ie checking plans against results and taking corrective actions, should also occur at several levels. Levels of planning provide a basis for control at different levels and by different responsible parties; it becomes possible to monitor both the project management and the experts responsible for specific activities in the project.

If the plan has to be revised as a consequence of changes in external conditions or because of internal project matters, it is an advantage if not every change requires the total re-planning of the project. When revisions are needed, it is beneficial to have planned the project at different levels. Global conditions in a project are more stable than the conditions upon which the activities are based. We should have a plan that allows changes at the activity level without having to change the whole plan; changes at the activity level can be introduced without any consequences for the plan at the management level. If there is only one comprehensive plan, there is a great danger that no one will be up to the effort of revising the whole plan when changes in details are made.

On the other hand, if changes are made in the basic conditions for the project, it is important to be able to show clearly how this will affect the plan at the global level. It must be possible to focus on the consequences for the project as a whole. Only then will the top executives and the line management get a clear picture of the changes and be able to decide on possible measures.

It is obviously essential to have a clear connection between plans at the two levels. It should be comparatively easy to translate the changes at the global level into changes at the activity level.

Basis for goal directed management

We argued above for two levels of planning. It is of utmost importance – and it is often neglected in practice to have a global plan. It is not sufficient to make only activity plans.

The planning at the global level should be concerned with what is to be accomplished and not how the work shall be done. In other words, this level must be goal oriented. In project work, it is quite impractical to operate solely with final goals. It is necessary to have certain checkpoints along the way. We call these checkpoints milestones.

It should be easy to ascertain whether or not a milestone has been reached. It is not always easy to formulate milestones in this way. But the easier it is to decide whether a milestone has been reached, the easier it becomes to control a project.

The milestones are checkpoints along the way in project work. Thus they have an important function in project management.

It is even better if the milestones also provide the organization and the line managers with useful results. The milestone then becomes both a checkpoint and a deliverable. We obtain what is called evolutionary development, a gradual fulfilment of project goals. The project does not wait until the last milestone to deliver all the results, but rather it plans to deliver results in instalments.

Binding plans

The plan at the global level (what we call the milestone plan) shows what the project shall deliver. The plan can be looked upon as a contract between the project owner and the project. It expresses the commitment undertaken by the project. The commitment rests first and foremost upon the project manager, but everyone involved in the project takes some responsibility.

This role given to the milestone plan corresponds to how organization plans are viewed in other areas of the organization. A marketing plan is a commitment on the part of the head of marketing and the marketing department to the top executives of the organization. It shows what results should be achieved in which markets for which products and to what extent. Like milestone plans, marketing plans do not contain information about activities. Plans for advertisements are not contained in marketing plans, for example, but are included in the internal planning documents in the marketing department.

The milestone plan is a commitment. This does not imply that it cannot be changed, but it means that changes must be made according to an established procedure, involving both the project owner and the project manager. To this end, the project should have a principle responsibility chart showing who must take decisions when the plan is subject to change.

The milestone plan shows the commitment assumed by the project. A prerequisite for this to be met is that the base organization makes the agreed resources available to the project at the right time. If the base organization does not fulfil its obligations, the project cannot meet its own. The commitments must be precisely described in order to avoid misunderstandings or different interpretations. When we liken commitments to contracts this emphasizes the importance of having them precisely formulated. The plan must thus show, as clearly as possible, which goals and intermediate goals (milestones) should be achieved. The base organization's commitment to the project must be expressed just as precisely in a principle responsibility chart.

SEGMENTATION OF PROJECT

Segmentation in general

Before starting a project it is wise to assess whether it is beneficial to divide the project into parts. There are several reasons for segmentation being advantageous. Figure 5.2 shows the most important grounds.

Decisions concerning the division of a project should be deferred until after the project's purpose has been established. Division must be determined in each individual case. What is considered a reasonable division will be strongly influenced by what the project is intended to do.

It is often expedient to divide a project to achieve a more manageable situation. A project that is large in terms of scope and duration might profit both administratively and managerially by being divided into several smaller projects. These advantages must be balanced against the disadvantage of being unable to manage all aspects of the task in one project.

A project may be maintained as a single unit, but be divided up into several sub-projects. Each sub-project will be a part of the

---

- The project is large
- The project is long term
- It is advantageous to have several parallel sub-projects subordinate to a main project
- We do not have the information to plan the whole project as one unit
- The project has several natural phases with completely different contents

Figure 5.2 Some important reasons for segmenting a project

main project. This simplifies administrative matters while at the same time the common connection to the main project allows the different tasks to be seen in relationship to each other. Sub-projects may be run consecutively or simultaneously.

A completely different reason for dividing a project is that it may not be possible to plan the whole project as one unit. The task may be such that information gathered and decisions taken at a certain stage of the project determine what milestones and activities should be carried out later in the project. As the conse-quences of the decisions are not yet fully known, there is no purpose to be served in drawing up a single overall plan. The last section of the plan will only consist of generalities because at the time the plan is made there is no certainty about what should be done during the later stages of the project.

Often, people draw up poor plans because they feel compelled to plan the whole project as one unit. They lack information, resulting in a poor plan that is useless for guidance and control. The project is highly likely to be unsuccessful.

Dividing the project into a feasibility phase (which may be called a preliminary project or feasibility study) and an imple-mentation phase (or main project) is one way of tackling this problem. In the feasibility study we describe problems more precisely, determine the purpose and goals of the project and take decisions on how to approach the problems. In the main project we implement what has been decided. In the next section we will examine more closely the distinction between these two kinds of projects.

The world, however, is not always so straightforward that it allows us to get the entire problem defining and solving out of the way first and then carry on with the implementation. In practice, problem resolution occurs on several levels, where we have both problem-defining activities and implementation activ-ities. Therefore, even in the main project there may be a need to analyse, evaluate and make decisions.

It is therefore appropriate to consider whether the project ought to be divided up into several smaller parts, which we call phases. This is relevant both in feasibility projects and imple-mentation projects. A characteristic of a phase is that it is possible to plan it as a whole. This means that planning can give us insight into the types of activities that should be done in this phase.

A product development project can naturally be divided into a number of different phases. There may be a phase for design and engineering, a phase for preparing the new product for production, a phase during which the product is introduced into the general production system, and a marketing phase. Some of these phases follow each other chronologically. It is not possible to prepare the product for production before completing the design and construction phase. On the other hand, it is not necessary to wait until the product is in production before starting the marketing phase. Planning for marketing can be initiated once the central decisions on design and engineering have been made. In this way market momentum is not lost.

Another project example improved the quality of the daily operations of the base organization which then led to ISO certification. The project started with a mapping and consciousness-raising phase, after which followed several parallel phases to improve quality in different areas.

A research programme on how to reduce pollution from livestock manure started with a traditional feasibility study (to discuss what should be researched). After that, five parallel sub-projects were started and scheduled to be conducted over a four-year period. They were to be concluded by delivering scientific reports. Two years before the scientific work was scheduled to be completed, a sub-project was started with the task of collating the information acquired thus far and developing recommendations on how farmers could reduce pollution. It was decided to release research results before all the scientific work had been completed because it was expected that there would be useful results to pass on to the agricultural industry.

When a project is divided into phases or sub-projects, it is necessary to discuss what goal each individual phase or sub-project is expected to achieve.

Feasibility study and implementation project

A feasibility study has different tasks from those of an implementation project. It should define precisely the objectives and goals of the project. It should work out what types of solutions can be used to achieve the goals, evaluate them and make further recommendations for an implementation project. The recommendations should be accompanied by financial plans and progress plans.

In the implementation project, tasks are decided upon to achieve the goals set forth in the feasibility study. In general, too little importance is given to feasibility studies. This applies to all types of projects and has serious consequences.

The starting point for a feasibility study is usually a project mandate. It outlines the problems or opportunities that form the background for starting the project. The goals for the project are formulated, but, as indicated previously, they can be fairly imprecise. Ideas for solutions to the problems or opportunities may also be found in the written material or verbal instructions that initiate the project.

Feasibility studies focus on formulating the goals. Imprecise and vague goals make later work in the project difficult and may cause project members to pull in different directions because they have different understandings of what the project is trying to achieve. Poorly formulated goals also greatly reduce the likelihood of a successful outcome.

A central task of a feasibility study is to identify possible alternative solutions that one has to choose from. If a feasibility study is not carried out or if the work is superficial, often one alternative (a certain solution) is selected without thorough analysis and evaluation. This is one of the main reasons that projects do not provide the base organization with the results it expects.

In a project intended to propose a computer solution for an administrative problem, it is crucially important that a feasibility study succeeds in finding and evaluating different types of solutions. Should the project develop the needed software itself? Should it buy a standard software package that can be installed without any alterations? Should it buy and then modify a standard software package?

Creativity is important in a feasibility study. If people are inventive in finding different possible solutions, they provide a good starting point for selecting the correct solution. A feasibility study must address the question of feasibility. The different possible solutions should thus be identified and the suitability of the alternatives should be evaluated as to their organizational, financial and technical feasibility. An assessment should be made to determine which alternative has the best chance of reaching the stated goals.

It can be seen from the above that there are two separate tasks that are dealt with in a feasibility study. The first works to define precisely what the project should achieve. The second identifies and evaluates alternative solutions. These two tasks may be represented as two phases in the feasibility study.

In the example regarding the IT system, the development of a requirement specification (showing what an IT solution should do for the organization) is the first phase, while selection of the particular software solution constitutes the second phase.

The main project (which is also called an implementation project) differs in character from a feasibility study. Creativity and analytical work are not at the forefront of a main project, but rather thoroughness, completeness and systematic work. It is important that all aspects of implementation are covered by the plans.

The feasibility study and the main project are planned separately. It is not realistic to plan the main project before the feasibility study has been completed. Planning of the main project may possibly be the final part of the feasibility study, in which case the mandate for the feasibility project would make it clear that this is included in its scope.

PRACTICAL MILESTONE PLANNING

Let us now suppose that we have progressed to a point in a project where we have described the project's purpose and its various goals. We may also have divided it into parts such as certain phases or sub-projects. We are tackling the first phase (or sub-project) in the project. We discuss what goals this phase should realize. Following this we can start drawing up a plan for this phase of the project.

Milestones

The plan will consist of several milestones and we shall show any dependencies between them. We call the plan a milestone plan. We will start by introducing the concept of milestone.

A milestone is a checkpoint in the project that ensures that we are on the right track. It is a description of a state the project should be in at a certain stage. It describes what the project should achieve, not how. As much as possible, a milestone should be neutrally stated in regard to ways of obtaining it.

We said that a milestone is a description of the state of the project at a certain stage. The word 'state' can be explained by giving some examples of 'everyday' states:

- being awake at 06:30;
- being at work 'on time';
- having achieved a planned result at work;
- having signed an important contract;
- having had a sale accepted;
- feeling full.

Such states can be described without indicating what activities have been performed to achieve them. We understand immediately that the state of being 'awake at 06:30' can be achieved with the help of several different types of activity, for example:

- You can go to bed early in order to wake up on your own.
- You can be awakened by an alarm clock.
- Another person can wake you up.
- You can stay up the whole night.

Similarly, the state of feeling 'full' can be achieved by going to a restaurant and eating, or by other activities such as shopping for food yourself, preparing the food and then eating it.

A state often means that a deliverable has occurred. 'Deliverable' means: a planned result, a signed contract, or perhaps an accepted sale.

There is a great difference between the following two examples in saying that a milestone has been reached: 'When the employees have specified knowledge in a stated area' versus 'When the members have completed course X'. The latter example is not neutral with regard to the output. Instead we have an activity-oriented formula. We have at an early planning stage tied ourselves to a specific activity (course X) instead of having the freedom at a later stage to choose the activities that could provide the employees with the desired knowledge. Neither does the latter formula allow quality control in the same way as a description of state. An employee may not necessarily have acquired particular knowledge even if the person concerned has participated in the course.

Most people, including project members, are not accustomed to thinking in terms of states. People are usually and mostly concerned with activities. Therefore, awareness is required when formulating milestones so that there is a real focus on states, and not on activities. Our point is that many different activities may lead to a certain state. Therefore, we choose to focus on the state first. Then later on, as part of the detailed planning, we would make a choice of necessary activities to achieve the state.

Milestone planning

We will return to the formulation of milestones, but first let us set up an example of a milestone plan with some milestones. Figure 5.3 shows a milestone plan.

The interpretation of such a plan is important. (In project literature there are several 'network plans', all having their own particular interpretation. It should not be assumed that because you have seen one kind of plan you know how to interpret them all.)

The milestone plan in Figure 5.3 should be understood as follows. In order to reach milestone M5 we must have been in the state described by milestone M4. Similarly, we cannot reach M4 before realizing M3, and so on. A milestone plan is a logical plan. It shows the logical dependencies relevant to the current project work.

In order to reach a specific milestone, a series of activities must have been completed. Some people believe that the milestone plan shows that the work involved in reaching one milestone cannot be started before the previous milestone has been

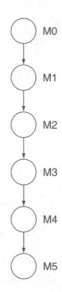

Figure 5.3 Milestone plan

reached. This is incorrect, and may be the result of conflicting interpretations from other types of network planning. In general, you do not need to wait until the previous milestone has been reached before starting to work on another. Figure 5.4 illustrates the relationship between activities and milestones.

Sometimes work on the next milestone cannot begin before the previous one has been reached. (The figure shows that work on M3 starts when M2 is reached and work on M4 starts when M3 is reached in this instance.) Work on a milestone may build directly upon the result achieved by the previous milestone, but most often it is either necessary or expedient to start working earlier on a milestone. Work on a specific milestone can commence while work on the previous one is in progress. (The figure illustrates this for milestone M2; work on it has started before M1 has been reached.) It may also be the case that work on a later milestone in the project starts before starting work on the preceding milestone in the series. (The figure shows that work towards M5 has started before work towards M3 and M4 has started.)

It is important to keep the essence of the milestone plan in mind; a milestone cannot be reached (work towards reaching this milestone cannot be completed) before the previous milestone

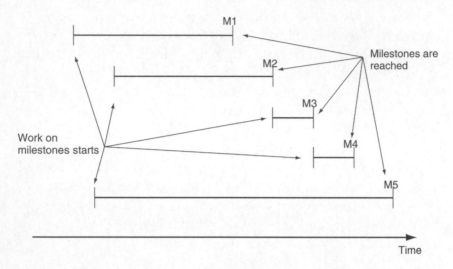

Figure 5.4 Correlation between activities and milestones

has been reached. It underlines the central point that the milestone plan is set up without taking any decisions on which activities must be started to reach the different milestones. This means that a milestone plan can be read and understood without having detailed insight into the underlying activities. For this reason also we call it a logical plan; it shows the logical dependencies between the states.

Experience shows that the milestone plan functions as an effective means of communication between the base organization and the project. It is important in this regard that line management feel they have a plan they can relate to. It shows, in a lucid manner, what the project is to achieve and the relationships between the different project milestones. We have often experienced people from the base organization discovering omissions and logical flaws in the milestone plan. This is a good indication that people understand the plan and its implications. It is also of importance that when the plan is accepted and understood by the line management, they too can use it as a means of control.

We have emphasized the significance of having a plan at the global level that does not have to be reassessed if changes occur at the activity level. Naturally, there is a particular need for this type of plan when working in unfamiliar areas where the necessary activities are not known in detail. The milestone plan remains in force even if it is decided to work forwards to a specific milestone by methods other than those originally considered. It is psychologically important for monitoring purposes to have a plan whose contents and appearance do not change for each reporting period. Frequent changes of a plan easily lead to monitoring being taken less seriously.

As a rule, a milestone plan is easy to read and understand. This does not imply that it is easy to draw up. Significant intellectual effort may be required to formulate a good milestone plan. We have already described it as a logical plan. This is because the making of a plan requires logical consideration of the states a project must pass through to achieve its goals.

Milestone plan for the project 'Excellent physical work environment'

Let us see what the milestone plan looks like for the project we introduced in the last section of Chapter 4. The project has been asked by the managing director in an organization (the project owner) to make an action plan to improve the physical work environment within the organization. A milestone plan for this project is shown in Figure 5.5.

The milestone plan shows that a description of the present situation should be developed first. It is important to note that the milestone plan does not say anything about how this should be done. For example, all employees or only a group of employees may be interviewed or sent questionnaires. No decision is taken at this stage on how to reach the milestone. What the project is to achieve should be determined first; then a discussion on how to achieve it can take place. Note that such a description of the present situation can be valuable in itself. It is advantageous to have a picture of the actual physical work environment. The milestone not only serves as a checkpoint in the work towards a completed project but it can also provide valuable information for the organization.

The next milestone requires a description of the desired situation. Work on developing a picture of the desired physical work environment may start before a description of the present situation

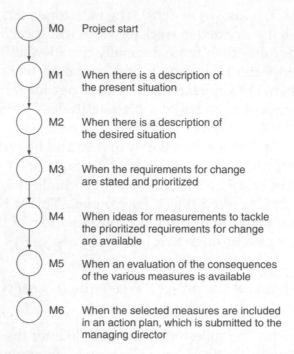

Figure 5.5 Milestone plan for the project 'Excellent physical work environment'

exists. It may, for example, be relevant to interview line managers and trade union representatives. A final description of the desired situation is not possible, however, before the description of the present situation has been completed; the description of the desired situation must take into account all the conditions mentioned in the description of the present situation.

The requirements for change will be the difference between the desired situation and the present situation. It is self-evident that it is impossible to obtain an overview of all the requirements for change and to prioritize them for action before obtaining the description of the desired situation. Ideas for measures to be taken must be generated, but at this stage we do not take any decisions on how to arrive at them. The consequences of the various measures must be evaluated and the best measures will be included in an action plan.

More about milestones

We have now presented the main ideas of the milestone plan. A good milestone plan requires well-formulated milestones. We will therefore examine in more detail what requirements we expect the milestones to meet. Figure 5.6 summarizes the important factors.

It is desirable that those who read and use the milestone plan should perceive the milestones as natural. What is considered natural obviously depends on the experience and knowledge in the area of work within which the project falls. Decisions traditionally regarded as being important in the current type of work are an example of natural milestones.

It is important for a milestone to be described in such a way that it is possible to ascertain that the desired state has been reached. This is the crux of this method of project management. It is impossible to have goal directed project management if it is not possible to check that an actual state has been reached.

It is easiest to confirm that a milestone has been reached when it concerns something visible that can be physically inspected. It is considerably more difficult with qualitative conditions: When has an organization become a better organization? How can we confirm that the environment has improved? It is possible to work on such qualitative conditions ad infinitum. It is therefore important to formulate the milestone in such a way that it describes some form of end point; it must indicate when the work can be considered completed and the result good enough.

In this context, it is significant to note that the formulation of a milestone may comprise two elements: a description of the desired situation (which we have stressed up to this point) and a description of the conditions attached to achieving this state. The conditions provide a precise expression of what must be done to

---

- A milestone text may often comprise two elements:
  - The state to be achieved
  - Conditions necessary to achieve the state
- A milestone should be controllable
- Important decision-making points in the project should be milestones
- Important deliverables in the project should be milestones

Figure 5.6 Some important requirements for milestones

ensure quality. In cases where it is not easy to control the quality of the desired state, it is all the more important to indicate what must be done before we can say that the desired state has been achieved.

The conditions provide the requirements for the desired quality of a milestone. A condition may refer to:

- methods that allow the result to be quality controlled;
- procedures (the intention is that the use of a specific procedure will ensure quality);
- previous work;
- professional approvals that need to be obtained (the intention is then that quality will be ensured by having a qualified person or qualified body approve the milestone).

Even if we use conditional elements in the milestone formulation, we try to adhere to the requirement of neutrality regarding the solution. Conditions should not suggest a detailed solution, but simply express which requirements must be met.

We will give some examples of milestone formulations. The sections referring to states in the milestones are in italics:

- *Suppliers are selected* on the basis of an approved purchasing procedure.
- *A proposal exists* and is approved by the managing director after a thorough review.
- *The description of administrative routines is available*, described with the help of PSO graphs.
- *Requirements for expertise and skills are met* after an approved training programme has been held.
- *Users have proved that they can manage independently* after the agreed training programme has been held.

The conditional element indicates the type of activities that must be carried out, or tools that must be used. We use this to ensure quality in a milestone, which is otherwise difficult to check for quality. However, the conditional element also makes it possible to limit the number of milestones and still make sure that the activities ensure quality takes place.

A milestone plan should provide an overview of the whole project. In order for this to occur, there should not be too many milestones. How many is a matter of judgement, but we believe that there should be fewer than 20. The maximum is perhaps about 15.

Use of milestones that are descriptions of states containing one or more conditions reduces the need for the number of milestones in a quality-oriented plan. The second milestone formulation listed above could have been divided into two parts: first, one that requires that the results of the review be documented, followed by another that requires that the boss to approve the proposal. In the last two formulations, we could have the completion of the training programme as a separate milestone.

Result paths

Until now we have shown a milestone plan where each milestone is only dependent on one other milestone. This is a rather one-dimensional plan, and not particularly typical of project work. A project usually addresses several needs or purposes in an organization; it usually has a composite goal, and the plan is therefore multi-dimensional. This means that several aspects of the project are worked on simultaneously.

In order to bring out the multi-dimensional aspects of project work, we introduce what we call a result path. A result path is a series of milestones that are closely related to each other. Milestones that contribute to the creation of a certain result form a result path. The links between the result paths show that works on the different types of results are interdependent. Figure 5.7 shows a milestone plan with result paths.

In this case the plan has three result paths. The number of paths in a plan depends on the nature of the project and how many major results are desired. We can thus have a plan with only one path. A plan with two to four paths is very common. More than four paths may introduce too much complexity.

Each path is given a name that describes what is going on in that part of the project. The first one or two letters in the designation may be included in a reference code to identify the milestones. In the figure the three result paths are called A, B and C. The milestones in path A are assigned the labels A1 and A2, the milestones in path B are called B1, B2, B3 and B4, and so on. We

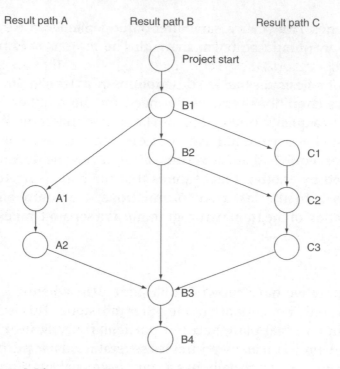

Figure 5.7 Milestone plan with result paths

can see from the milestone plan that milestone A2 cannot be reached before A1 has been reached. As we saw in the simplest plans, there is a dependent relationship between milestones in an individual result path. We can also see, however, that neither A1 nor C1 can be reached before B1 has been realized. B3 requires that both B2 and C3 are reached. Thus the plan also shows dependencies between the paths. Work on one type of project result may depend upon what needs to be achieved in other result areas.

Milestone B4 is the end milestone in this project. It has an important position in a project, but realization of the project goals should not rest on this milestone alone. It is a positive and useful factor if some goals have already been realized via previous milestones. For example, it may be that the achievement of A2 means that the goals linked to the part of the project covered by result path A have been reached. C3 may play a corresponding role for result path C. And it may even be that certain goals have already been achieved at earlier project milestones. In any case, realization of B4 means that all the project goals have been achieved, giving the final milestone a special significance.

A very important aspect of planning is to define good result paths. They tell the readers of the plan what results the project aims to achieve.

Goals for the project can be used as a starting point to define result paths in the milestone plan. A goal expresses precisely what we want to achieve and the specific type of result. Therefore, goals are suitable as the basis for dividing the plan into result paths. If three main goals have been set for a project, they often provide a starting point for three different result paths in the plan.

Before making a final decision on the result paths, other matters should be taken into consideration such as whether the project needs to focus on any specific problems, or whether there are any conditions especially critical for success. For example, we might consider quality assurance to be a critical success factor. In that case, we might make quality assurance a result path. We might also make building support for the project in the base organization a result path because it is of vital importance for the project's success. In general, however, it is best to use the goals as the basis for setting up result paths. Attention should then be paid to such matters as quality and support in connection with each individual milestone.

An organization wished to install a new local area network for its data processing. In the project set up, the first phase was to select a network. The purpose of the network was to support the users' requirements for data processing services. It had to be cost effective, and it had to meet requirements for security and accessibility. Four result paths were selected: Choice of network, User requirements, Finance, and Security/accessibility. The result paths show very clearly what was important for the project; they show the professional focus areas of the project.

Milestone plan for the project 'Excellent physical and social work environment'

In our first example of a milestone plan (Figure 5.5) we had only one result path. The project task was to draw up an action plan to improve the physical work environment in an organization. We have an expansion of scope if the managing director also requests the project to improve the social work environment in addition to improving the physical work environment. With this scope and goals formulated for both the physical and social work environments, it is natural to suggest one result path for the physical environment and one for the social environment. Work on the milestone plan will probably reveal dependencies between these two paths. However, a closer look may reveal that three result paths will be better. The third one may represent general actions addressing matters of relevance both to the physical and social work environment. The new milestone plan is shown as Figure 5.8.

We see from the milestone plan that social matters should be addressed before the physical conditions are. Highlighting these types of logical relationships is a great strength of milestone planning.

This brief example also illustrates how result paths communicate in terms that the project owner and the base organization can understand because it shows that the project is working on matters they want to be solved.

Forming the milestone plan

The following is advice on how to do milestone planning in practice. We emphasize that milestone planning is group work. It is important that a sense of community develops around the plan. It is also important that various types of expertise required for the project be involved.

For group work to function well, physical conditions must be favourable. Everyone must have a fair opportunity to participate actively. One possibility is to use a flip chart. Everyone can see what is written on the large sheets of paper and it is easy to use different colours. A further point is that the sheets can be torn off when they are covered with text and symbols, and hung up around the room. The sheets should 'decorate' the room so that it is easy to keep a continuous overview of all the ideas contributed by the participants.

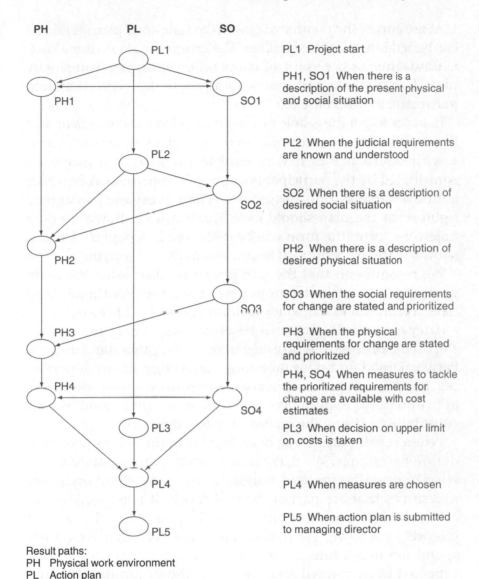

PH   PL   SO

PL1 Project start

PH1, SO1 When there is a description of the present physical and social situation

PL2 When the judicial requirements are known and understood

SO2 When there is a description of desired social situation

PH2 When there is a description of desired physical situation

SO3 When the social requirements for change are stated and prioritized

PH3 When the physical requirements for change are stated and prioritized

PH4, SO4 When measures to tackle the prioritized requirements for change are available with cost estimates

PL3 When decision on upper limit on costs is taken

PL4 When measures are chosen

PL5 When action plan is submitted to managing director

Result paths:
PH   Physical work environment
PL   Action plan
SO   Social work environment

Figure 5.8 Milestone plan for the project 'Excellent physical and social work environment'

Another possibility is that everyone writes down a proposal for milestones on 'Post-It' slips (slips with an adhesive strip on the reverse side, so they can be positioned and then moved as necessary). This allows participants to discuss the dependencies between different milestones and their positions in result paths and illustrate points by moving the slips on which the milestones are noted.

At the end of the planning session, the milestone plan should be converted into a finished outline. The group should do this also. It is damaging to the spirit of cooperation if one person sits by himself in a corner and draws up a proposal. Everyone should participate in this phase too.

In order to get the whole group involved in the conversion to a finished outline, we recommend the use of a whiteboard. Using a whiteboard makes it very easy to integrate the proposals contributed by the participants into a milestone plan. A flip chart is not suitable during this phase. When everyone has agreed upon what the plan should look like, it can be drawn up on a milestone form (the form will be discussed in Chapter 11 and is shown in the Appendix). It is simply a matter of copying.

We recommend that the group start by discussing the main goals as presented in the project mandate. It is important that all have a common understanding of the goals of the project.

After this, result paths can be discussed. This is an essential step in the process. It is no exaggeration to say that the difference between good and poor milestone plans often lies in determining good result paths. It is also important to name the paths appropriately. Experience has shown us that good names contribute to raising the quality of milestone plans.

When result paths have been agreed upon, we can begin to define milestones. We may work on each path separately. It is wise to describe the end milestone first and then any other milestones that are part of the end result. It is important that everyone has the same understanding of what the project intends to achieve. We recommend, however, that we do not spend too much time on the end milestone because it can be expected to be refined later on when the group has acquired better insight into, and understanding of, the project. Indeed, the project's various goals can be achieved in several ways and are not connected solely to the end milestone.

We can then seek out relevant milestones more freely. The group needs to do a great deal of work to formulate each milestone. It is easy to underestimate the value of this work, but it is important that each member gains an understanding of both the project work to be carried out and the task of controlling the project.

During the discussion of milestones, proposals for activities will arise. Discussing activities should not distract the main discussion, but it is important that the activities mentioned are noted so that they can be discussed later on. If we discuss activities too much at this stage, the milestone plan will often become activity oriented, and not state oriented as we wish it to be. Nevertheless, certain activities can provide ideas for milestones, and therefore it is undesirable to ban totally the mentioning of activities.

Evaluation of the milestone plan

Upon completing a draft of the milestone plan it is necessary to carry out a comprehensive evaluation of it.

Firstly, is the plan balanced? It should have approximately the same degree of detail throughout. Some parts should not be significantly more detailed than others. If the first part of the project is planned in great detail and the final part is so rough and diffuse that people can hardly determine what the milestones represent, it is likely that the planning horizon was too distant. How far into the future we should plan and whether the plan should be divided into several plans is discussed in the next section.

Secondly, does the milestone plan have good result paths? We have already stressed the importance of suitable result paths. They should reflect the purpose and the goals of the project and show the areas within which the results are to be achieved. People in the base organization should be able to understand immediately what each individual path represents. In principle, all result paths should have milestones throughout most of the milestone plan. Result paths should not end early in the milestone plan. This indicates either an incorrect choice of result path or missing milestones.

Thirdly, is the milestone plan logical? People who did not draw up the plan should check the plan's logical construction. Detailed knowledge of project activities should not be required for people to review the plan. Everyone who needs to be involved in it should easily understand the milestone plan. Top management and line management should not accept a plan that they cannot understand.

Fourthly, are the milestones suitable? The milestone formulations must also be checked according to the requirements that we defined earlier. Basically, a milestone should express a desired state to be reached.

Fifthly, and finally, is the milestone plan an overview plan? A milestone plan should fit on one page. This is important to help everyone have an overview of the project. Even plans that are only two pages in length are not as easy to comprehend. Every once in a while we hear the assertion 'it is not possible to draw up a one-page plan for our project'. We have yet to find an instance where this is true. It is always possible to draw up a rational and serviceable milestone plan on one page. In some cases milestones have to be combined. We do have an upper limit for the number of milestones that there can be in one plan. This might cause worry that the plan will not then include all the states the project must logically go through. However, we can link several conditions to the milestones selected, and thus cover what must be done before each milestone is reached.

One or several milestone plans?

In general, we say that you should not plan any further forward than is practical, but what is practical varies from project to project. In many projects, decisions are made during the initial planning stage that determine the direction of the project and the type of work that will actually be carried out in the final stages. It is not particularly practical to plan the whole project at once, when at the time of planning you do not know what the latter sections of the project will deal with and what kind of work will then be relevant. It is inappropriate, and a way of deceiving yourself and others, to draw up a plan where the final stages consist solely of generalities because you do not know what tasks will be involved.

This is an unfamiliar concept for many project managers. They realize that it is practical to divide a project into a feasibility study and a main project. Many, however, do not realize that it may also be necessary to further divide the project into phases with separate plans for each phase.

A PSO project is characterized by the fact that the choice of the project's direction and approach should depend on a maturation process in the earliest stages of the project involving learning and the development of attitudes. In such cases it is inappropriate to start the project by establishing what should occur later on. Drawing up one plan for the whole project is not recommended. Instead there is a need for several consecutive plans.

In projects where a proposal is to be submitted in reply to an invitation to tender, the situation forces you to plan the whole project as one unit. In such cases requirements must be set at the outset for what will actually be executed in the later phases. In purely technical projects, where you have a good idea about most of the actual project activities, this may not cause difficulties. In a PSO project this type of overall plan can prove to be a considerable hindrance to rational work later in the project. When the plan begins to appear inadequate, you may decide to stick to it and make silly mistakes. Or you can deviate from it, choose a new direction that you now understand to be best, but be criticized because you did not follow the plan.

Result paths vary from phase to phase in a project. The reason for this, of course, is that the results we create in one phase will be essentially different from those created in another phase. There are, for example, always different result paths for a feasibility study and for a main project.

A light-fitting factory wanted to develop a range of fittings that would be better designed and more functional than earlier products. At the same time, the products would have to be profitable. In the milestone plan there was one result path for the design, another for functionality, and a third for profitability. It is self-evident that after the first phase is completed and the design and functionality have been worked out, these elements will not be relevant result paths in further work.

We earlier referred to a project that was to select a computer network. Four result paths were selected: choice of network, user requirements, finance, and security/accessibility. The result paths of the implementation phase may be based on PSO and will be quite different from the four above. There might be a result path for people development (training and motivation), one for the technical part (implementation of the hardware and software) and one for organizational development (implementation of new procedures and responsibilities).

6

Global organizing – milestone responsibility chart

In this chapter we will first present our views on how a project should be organized. For PSO projects we recommend the matrix organizational structure (project work is integrated with the base organization). A responsibility chart is a tool that makes it possible to take advantage of the positive aspects of the matrix structure (the second section gives a general description of a responsibility chart, while the third section presents the milestone responsibility chart, that is, the tool we use for organizing project work at the global level). We then illustrate how to time schedule a project. At the end of this chapter, we discuss how to conduct uncertainty analysis at the global level. The analysis is based on the milestone plan and the milestone responsibility chart.

PRINCIPLES OF PROJECT ORGANIZATION

Project work often requires participation by people who are not usually accustomed to this type of work. When they take part in project work they only spend a portion of their working hours on it; that is to say, they are not 100 per cent occupied with project activities. Work of this nature and type of effort must be organized in a certain way if the project work is to be completed without stumbling into pitfalls. Our views on important aspects of organizing project work follow.

Integrating project work and the base organization

When a project has to be organized, you quickly encounter the following problem. Should people participating in project work be released fully from their other daily duties for a project's duration and physically relocate to a 'project room'? Or, while they work on the project, should they still occupy their normal workstation and divide their time between project work and daily duties?

Figure 6.1 illustrates the problem. Both solutions have their advantages and their drawbacks.

The advantage of releasing people from other tasks and moving them to a 'project room', represented by A in Figure 6.1, is that the project member can concentrate completely on project

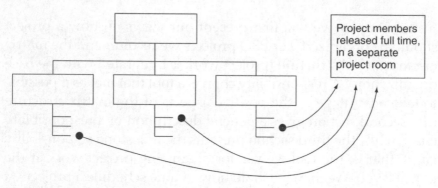

A) Project members are released from their daily work and moved

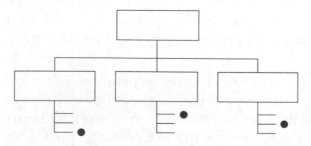

B) Project tasks are executed along with daily work. Project members remain at their desks working in their normal environment

Figure 6.1 Two different ways of organizing project work when involving project members from the base organization

work. Nothing else distracts him and he is able to concentrate fully on the project. When people are moved to a project room, it usually does not take very long before they see things from the project's point of view and lose the perspective of the base organization. For example, when user representatives are included in a computer systems development project on a full-time basis, they often very quickly become 'computer people' and begin to talk 'computerese'. This is one of alternative A's drawbacks. The project members cease to be concerned with the very interests that they are expected to represent. Another drawback is poor utilization of resources, especially in projects where progress depends on decisions from the base organization. Since project members no longer work so closely with their home location, these decisions are often delayed.

A solution involving a division of time between project tasks and daily tasks is termed 'integration of the project work and the base organization', and is represented by B in Figure 6.1. The advantage of B is that in principle the whole base organization is at its disposal for project tasks. Not having to pull people out of the base organization to perform project tasks gives greater flexibility. The project can concentrate on finding the people who have the best qualifications for the tasks and a larger number of people can be involved in the work. Some may do a very limited amount of work while others may work nearly full-time.

In alternative B, the project is regarded to a greater extent as the responsibility of the base organization. Project members remain at their own desks and do not lose their links with their usual job and their area of expertise. Integration of project work into the base organization requires gaining acceptance of the fact that development tasks (projects) are also an important activity for people who have a job in the ordinary base organization. This integration generally leads to a more positive attitude towards development work in the base organization.

When the project is integrated, there is an additional tendency for people other than the individual project members to become engaged in project problems and progress. Often, project members discuss their problems and successes with their colleagues, producing increased involvement in the project. Alternative B also makes it easier for a project member to discuss some matters with colleagues. The probability of an informal hearing is greater when people have easy access to colleagues. If someone is taken out of the base organization, completely different procedures must be used to gather opinions from his original environment.

Alternative B provides a more effective use of resources. It is easier to utilize spare time if you are in your normal work environment. You can simply turn to your other duties. A danger in alternative A is that the project manager may attempt to fill free time by assigning tasks that are not ready to be done or assigning tasks to a person not qualified to carry them out.

You can deduce from this that we are in favour of alternative B. However, we do not deny that it may be difficult to implement. An absolutely essential prerequisite is to define, detail, and gain agreement on responsibilities and authorities in advance. It is unrealistic to believe that integration of project work into the base organization will be achieved without this.

We recommend that three particularly important factors be evaluated before integrating project work into the base organization:

- The line manager's qualities: it is especially important to assess whether the line manager will be able to organize his department in such a way that project members can be relieved of their normal operational tasks to the extent agreed upon.
- The project members' qualities: an assessment must be made as to whether project members will be able to handle their normal tasks and project tasks while giving the agreed priority to the project. Some people need to be supervised constantly; if not, they will always be fully occupied with their normal job and neglect their project work.
- The attitudes of the base organization: at the outset there must be acceptance in the base organization of the fact that colleagues will spend a certain amount of their time on project work. Without this acceptance, the environment will hamper the project members' ability to perform their project tasks. Customers, colleagues, and/or management will never allow them the necessary time to do the project work. Colleagues must also agree to relieve the project members of some of their normal duties. When a project member

performs project work in the base organization, all his colleagues must be restricted from disturbing him with daily matters.

We believe that alternative B is the best for PSO projects. Close contact between the project and the base organization is required. This is not as important for large technical projects with their huge need for resources (most project members working full-time).

Principal organizational matters before details

When organizing a project, we are concerned with the question of who should perform various project tasks. Of course, it is important to fill all the roles in a project with able people. However, as in planning project work, there is a tendency to become too quickly involved in discussing the details (in this case choice of personnel) before the global principles are made clear. Separating the definition of global principles for participation and roles of various parties involved in the project from actual allocation of tasks to specific people is an important aspect of good planning.

In discussing principles, decisions are made about what role different parties will play in the project. In this discussion, the project, the base organization and other parties involved agree upon the 'rules of the game'. Such discussions of principle are especially important when the project will draw on resources from the base organization. (This applies to most projects, apart from huge projects where everyone is engaged full-time on the project.) This is particularly important when the project work is integrated into the base organization. It is necessary to clarify the organization's responsibility and participation in the project and this must be done before we begin to consider specific people for the project tasks.

Clarification of all roles and responsibilities

Every project has relationships to many different parties. Examples of these parties are the project owner, the users of the project results (both line management and end users) and other interested bodies (for example, a trade union).

For example, in a PSO project that is developing a computer-based ordering and invoicing system the parties involved are the organization's top management, the finance director (the 'user boss'), members of the finance department (the users), members of the computer department (different types of experts), trade unions, and the organization's major suppliers and customers. When organizing the project, both the principles governing relationships between the parties involved and the practical consequences of these relationships must be defined. It must be clear who will make the different types of decisions, who should be informed, and who should perform the different types of work. Through such careful definition, organizational pitfalls can be avoided.

In a traditional project organization, terms of responsibility and authority are usually described for those who are formally connected to the project. However, the importance of clarifying relationships with external parties involved with the project is often neglected when setting up a project.

Defining decision-making responsibilities

Part of organizing a project is to clarify the types of decisions various parties involved will take. We maintain, as a principal point of departure, that decisions should be taken by those in the base organization who are normally responsible for these kinds of decisions.

If a computer-based invoicing system is to be drawn up, it may contain rules for discounts for premium customers. The people in the base organization who have daily responsibility for determining this sort of thing must formulate these. Why should the right to make this type of decision be transferred to a steering committee, a project group or some computer people because the work of developing and implementing the new system is organized as a project? The person responsible for the area of concern should be responsible for taking decisions that affect that area, and he should do this by virtue of his job in the base organization. However, these demands on the line manager or his subordinates must be defined and agreed upon when setting up the project. Otherwise there is a great danger that the project will usurp the power to make decisions. The consequence of this is that at a later stage the base organization will rightly deny responsibility for the system, because they will point to the fact that the project has made the decisions that should have been made by the base organization.

There is always a tendency for a project steering committee to become a project decision group and make decisions that it does not have the qualifications or the right to make. We strongly reject the idea that such a group function as decision-makers concerning professional questions. A project must not deprive the base organization of its responsibility for making profession-ally related decisions.

Communicating effectively

In some projects, the problem of information is resolved by disseminating 'mountains' of information about the project to anyone who may be considered to have an interest in it. The problem of consultation is resolved by assembling people in reference groups. For fear of treading on someone's toes, too many are included in these groups. The consequences are meet-ings with many people present who are not responsible for, or have no connection with, the problems discussed. Reference groups often serve as a form of collective hostage.

We recommend more careful consideration of who should be consulted and informed. The project should analyse the benefits it intends to achieve against the administrative costs needed to undertake the dissemination of information. It is better to have some in-depth discussions with individuals than superficial discussions in a large reference group.

Flexibility

In many projects, a project group will be formally appointed consisting of a group of people who will carry out the work involved in the project. These people are there from start to finish, and will perform all the large and small tasks in the project. If we have a project organization in which people are formally assigned to a project for its lifetime, we may face the following dangers:

- difficulty in varying the input of resources during the life-time of the project;
- precluding the best people from the base organization for certain tasks;
- creating a gap between those who are formally included in the project and those who are not.

It is important to organize a project in such a way as to allow flexibility in acquiring different types of resources at different stages of the project. We call this an 'accordion' organization. At the same time, it is important that we state precisely what each individual is to do.

With an accordion organization we can achieve the following:

- The number of people working on a project can vary during its lifetime. This is advantageous because during the course of a project the requirement for an input of resources and different types of expertise varies considerably.
- The 'right' expertise is crucial when allocating tasks, and we have a better chance of getting this expertise when the project is organized flexibly. If project members are formally appointed to cover all project work, we are prevented from using the most competent people in the base organization when needed. Of course, even with a formally appointed project group we can still get help from people outside the project. However, they are not a part of the project in the same formal way. When they agree to do a job, they often do it as an act of friendship; we are dependent on their good-will. It is important that everyone working on a project has the same status within it.
- Participation in the project always depends on whether or not the person in question is presently doing a job for the project. A flexible form of organization means that participation in the project is in a constant state of flux. Permanent appointments create rigidity and management difficulties. The project will be obliged to hang on to people who no longer have anything to contribute. We have yet to see an internal memo stating that a person is leaving the formal project group and is no longer participating in a project.

An accordion organization does not mean that no one can work full-time on the project. The project manager and his closest allies may be allocated 100 per cent to the project. They may form the core team of the project.

RESPONSIBILITY CHARTS

Purpose

The project organization should be 'tailor-made' to resolve the project task. Because every project is unique, it is important that an organization be specially formulated for each individual project. It should be as suitable as possible with regard to the task to be performed.

To reiterate, when organizing we should pay attention to the important matters briefly summed up as follows. We must have an accordion organization in which people are included in a project only as long as they have tasks to perform. We must always observe the principle that the right to make decisions on professionally related questions belongs to those who have daily responsibility for them. Project work must be integrated into the base organization. The right people must be consulted and informed.

Our method of organizing projects requires a thorough discussion of what the people involved in the project (project owner, project management, project members, line management, users, shop stewards, etc) will do. Discussions on organization must occur at two levels, ie the clarification of organizational principles before dealing with detailed matters.

Establishing a 'tailor-made' project organization requires that a fundamental stance be taken on what roles the various parties involved should play in the project at the global level. The 'rules of the game' that will apply to the project should be clarified. Detailed organization comes at a later stage and requires clarification of concrete activities to be performed and the commitment of specific people to the different activities.

Both the global discussion and the detail discussion will be held with the help of a tool that we call a responsibility chart. It is inspired by the matrix model and is sometimes called a responsibility matrix or a responsibility contract. Responsibility charts are constructed in the same way whether they are at the global level in the form of the principle responsibility chart or the milestone responsibility chart, or at the detailed level in the form of an activity responsibility chart. But the charts clarify different types of questions. The principle responsibility chart describes and clarifies the division of responsibilities in important project matters between the project and the base organization. The milestone responsibility chart explains and describes the roles of different parties necessary to achieve the different milestones of the project. The activity responsibility chart explains and describes the roles of specific people in concrete project activities. Figure 6.2 illustrates a responsibility chart.

Roles

The responsibility chart is also used to clarify roles. The roles are the same at all levels. Figure 6.3 shows different roles and abbreviations that will be used on the responsibility chart.

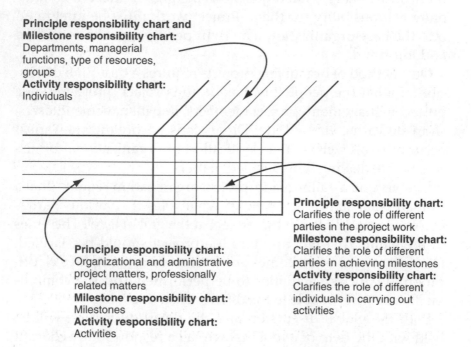

Principle responsibility chart and Milestone responsibility chart:
Departments, managerial functions, type of resources, groups
Activity responsibility chart:
Individuals

Principle responsibility chart:
Organizational and administrative project matters, professionally related matters
Milestone responsibility chart:
Milestones
Activity responsibility chart:
Activities

Principle responsibility chart:
Clarifies the role of different parties in the project work
Milestone responsibility chart:
Clarifies the role of different parties in achieving milestones
Activity responsibility chart:
Clarifies the role of different individuals in carrying out activities

Figure 6.2 Responsibility chart

X	Executes the work
D	Takes decisions solely or ultimately
d	Takes decisions jointly or partly
P	Manages work and controls progress
T	Provides tuition on the job
C	Must be consulted
I	Must be informed
A	Available to advise

Figure 6.3 Roles in a project identified on the responsibility chart, with their abbreviations

We will discuss different roles that are assignable as part of the organizing process.

It is vital to be able to mark who should 'do the work', ie execute a specific task. It is important to manage and administer the project well, but in the end it is the quality of execution that matters most. We must clarify who has the responsibility for executing the different tasks of the project.

We can also state who will make decisions on matters of importance. We use two different decision symbols for principal and subsidiary decision-making. A problem can very often be divided and the authority to make decisions can be divided accordingly. For example, a problem can be divided into the person who makes the principal decision (or 'has the final word') and others who are responsible for making decisions on the subsidiary problems. The division into major decisions and subsidiary decisions makes it possible for upper management to hand over subsidiary decisions to others.

In certain cases the decision symbols stand for professional approval. We have not found it necessary to have a separate symbol for this. This is evident from the context when a decision is made and when the situation is more a case of professional approval.

Figure 6.4 further illustrates the use and interpretation of the decision symbols. We stress that there should not be two capital 'D's on the same line, except for cases in which the project is a joint effort between two or more independent organizations. There is only one person in an organization who can have the overall responsibility for a decision. However, there may well be several lower-case 'd's on the same line. If there are only

	Party X	Party Y	Party Z	Explanation
Example I	D			X has full responsibility for the decision
Example II	D	d		Y answers for professional quality and gives approval within his field. X has full responsibility for the deci-sion
Example III	D	d	d	Y and Z agree jointly, but X makes the formal decision
Example IV		d	d	If Y and Z agree jointly, their decision stands. If not, the decision is taken at a higher level in the manage-ment hierarchy

Figure 6.4 Use of decision symbols in a responsibility chart

lower-case 'd's – without a capital 'D' – it means that the 'd' people must agree and make decisions jointly. If, on the other hand, in addition to lower-case 'd's there is a capital 'D', it implies that the 'D' person is included in the decision-making process and has the final responsibility.

On the responsibility chart, one can show whether a group or an individual 'must be consulted' by using the 'C' symbol. This does not mean that the person concerned has veto powers, but that it is a very serious mistake if the person concerned is not allowed to express his views. This symbol is often used to describe the role of a trade union representative. He too does not have the authority to make decisions or veto power, but it is important to listen to his opinions when decisions are to be made.

'Available for advice' is used for several reasons. It is used to open up channels of communication in extremely formal surroundings. An 'A' implies the formal opportunity to 'pester' people. Those involved understand that they can be contacted to discuss problems. The symbol can also be used to indicate people with particular expertise to draw upon so that their advice is not overlooked. Accountants are a good example of this. People who are assigned the 'A' symbol thus receive a formal role in the project. This symbol can be particularly important to external consultants involved in a project. It gives these consultants a right to make contact with people in the base organization without having to ask someone for permission. Gathering information and establishing contact can be otherwise difficult for consultants who come from outside the organization. If 'available for advice' is indicated for an external consultant, it implies that the project has a 'green light' for them to use.

The 'I' symbol designates 'Must be informed'. This is important because it indicates who should be informed about the matter.

Responsibility for work and progress is marked with a capital 'P'. In project work, we are constantly struggling to achieve high quality and to keep within time and budget limits. This responsibility for progress is especially important and includes the management functions of planning, organization and control. There should always be one and only one capital 'P' on each line of the responsibility chart indicating only one person to take responsibility for the progress of the task concerned.

We can indicate responsibility for transfer of knowledge with a capital 'T'. It involves a combination of leadership and support when performing the work. At the start of a task, the people who will perform it do not always have the expertise to do it on their own, and must acquire this expertise. For example, when people must use a special investigation or descriptive technique during the course of the work and they don't initially have adequate knowledge of it, we should assign someone to provide the necessary training and support.

In general, we suggest that you should be sparing in the use of symbols on responsibility charts. If the responsibility chart is 'showered' with symbols, a lengthy project may be the consequence. In such cases there should be a new round of discussions on the responsibility chart to decide whether such broad involvement is really appropriate. If broad involvement is deemed desirable, then everyone should expect this to slow down the progress of the project.

Developing the responsibility charts at the foundation, global, and detail levels requires thorough discussion. The responsibility chart gives a condensed description of what has been agreed upon. Sometimes, there is a need to supplement the responsibility chart with a verbal discussion that describes, in more depth, the significance of the individual symbols in the matrix.

The resulting project organization design is important; however, the clarification process that must take place to produce it is just as important. In organizational work all parties involved at the foundation and principal level and all individuals involved at the detail level must be included. Each party's relationship to the project must are clarified in the discussions. Any disagreements on the understanding of, or expectations as to, individual roles should be resolved. This will not eradicate all conflicts in a project, but undoubtedly, a range of problems that could break out later in the form of open conflict may be prevented at an early stage.

Lastly, not the least benefit is that participants will develop a stronger loyalty and identification to the project while they cooperate in the organizing of it.

MILESTONE RESPONSIBILITY CHART – RESPONSIBILITIES FOR ACHIEVING MILESTONES

The milestone plan of the project shows how the project will progress in a global sense. It presents, in an easily understandable way, what the project shall deliver. The crucial question is: Who should be responsible for actually achieving the different milestones in the milestone plan? The milestone responsibility chart gives the answer.

The milestone responsibility chart can be regarded as a contract between the project and the parties involved. It is important in this contract to agree upon the relationships between those involved and the project, and that the 'frontiers' between those involved are staked out where necessary. In a project, management and members from the base organization are drawn in. For the project to be successful it is necessary that all parties involved in the base organization understand clearly what responsibilities they have, and accept them explicitly.

A quite natural extension of milestone planning is the discussion about who should be responsible for the different milestones. In practice, we take each milestone in turn, discuss them, decide upon which parties should play a role in achieving them, and agree upon the role of those parties.

Milestone responsibility chart for the project 'Excellent physical work environment'

We showed earlier the milestone plan for the project 'Excellent physical work environment' (Figure 5.5). We will now show in Figure 6.5 what the milestone responsibility chart might look like for this project.

In a milestone plan, each milestone is formulated as a description of a state, possibly with certain conditions attached. It is the work leading up to the milestone that will be regulated on the responsibility chart. We do not, therefore, repeat the whole milestone formula. We can select a formulation that clearly shows that it is the work up to the milestone that we are looking at. Or we can use keywords from the milestone and let it be understood that the responsibility chart applies to the responsibility for achieving that milestone.

Milestone M1 is called 'When there is a description of the present situation'. On the milestone responsibility chart it says 'Description of present situation'. These are keywords from the complete milestone formulation. 'Describe the present situation' could also be entered there. Such a term indicates more clearly

	Project manager	Managing director	Affected line managers	Personnel consultant	Work environment committee	External consultant
M1 Description of present situation	X/P	A	C	X	X	T
M2 Description of desired situation	X/P	D	d	X	C	
M3 Requirements for change	X/P			X	I	
M4 Ideas for measures	X/P		C	X	C	A
M5 Consequences of the measures	X/P		X		I	
M6 Action plan	X/P		C	X	C	

Figure 6.5 Milestone responsibility chart for the project 'Excellent physical work environment'

that it is the responsibility for the work to achieve the milestone that will be agreed upon.

Some milestones say something about who should make decisions, or who should confirm that a milestone has been achieved. It is unnecessary to repeat this in the keywords on the responsibility chart because this is exactly what the responsibility chart shows – eg where the authority to make decisions lies.

Now and again, it is necessary to divide a milestone into two or more sections on the responsibility chart because the authority relationships are so different. If the milestone work is seen as one unit, these differences are not perceived.

In the above example we could have divided M5 'Consequences of the measures' into two parts, one part called 'Economic consequences of the measures' and another part called 'Consequences of the measures on the work environment'. The responsibility chart could thus have shown that the parties participating in the work on investigating the economic consequences will not be the same as those who investigate the effects on the work environment. In the example we have not gone into the tasks in great depth; in practice this is often necessary.

More on forming the milestone responsibility chart

The milestone responsibility chart shows what responsibility the different parties have for achieving the milestones. This responsibility can thus consist of being responsible for progress, executing work, making decisions, being available for consultation, receiving information or tutoring. A party may well have several roles simultaneously. It is usual, for example, at least in smaller projects that the person responsible for progress also participates in doing actual project work.

It is sometimes difficult to find suitable terms for the parties involved, especially when responsibility will be assigned to a group of people who are not usually regarded as forming one unit. The attainment of a milestone may, for example, require a specific effort from certain, but not all, line managers. In such cases the group may be called 'affected line managers', 'specific line managers' or something similar.

In the example (Figure 6.5) we see that affected line managers 'must be consulted' in the description of the present situation. This means that the head of production must make a statement on the actual situation in the production department, the head of marketing on the situation in the marketing department, the head of personnel on the situation in the personnel department, etc. When it is stated that the affected line manager should make a subsidiary decision on the desired situation, it means that the head of production will decide on matters for his department, the head of marketing for his, and so on. But we see that the managing director makes the principal decision. This means that the managing director has the right to reconsider whatever the line managers have decided.

It is important to realize that one person may be included in several parties. For example, one person may be both an elected employee representative and an affected user. The responsibilities attached to each of these functions are essentially different, and this may lead to the person being assigned different types of work on the basis of his affiliation with different groups.

During work on the milestone responsibility chart an evaluation of the milestone plan will take place. If there are any logical flaws, problems may occur in filling in the responsibility chart. It may indeed be the case that work on the responsibility chart will lead you to return to, reassess, and alter the milestone plan.

Discussing responsibilities is not an easy process. It is important, as we also said in connection with the development of the milestone plan, to arrange matters practically so that all participants can engage in a genuine group discussion. We pointed out earlier that the use of a whiteboard in presentations ensures that everyone can follow the discussion towards agreement. In addition, this tool makes it easy to note changes.

We usually recommend that the discussion about roles and responsibilities start by considering the first three or four milestones and the different parties involved. If there are no problems, then all the subsequent milestones can be set up. The reason that we recommend that you start with a few milestones is that it can be difficult to establish which parties should be included on the responsibility chart, and it is unnecessary to discuss all the milestones before you feel that you have found the right ones.

When the milestone responsibility chart has been developed, it is useful to evaluate the results. Two types of analyses can be made: horizontal analysis and vertical analysis.

In the horizontal analysis each milestone is reviewed individually and the work to achieve each one is evaluated. You should assess whether the roles have been correctly balanced and integrated for the milestone. We have emphasized earlier that there must be one person who is responsible for managing progress. It is easy to check whether this requirement is satisfied. There are larger problems in determining whether there is sufficient skill and expertise among those executing the work. You might assess at this point whether there is a need for on-the-job training and whether the right advice can be obtained from those whom one can or must consult. The group must consider whether decisions are held at the right level. It must also determine whether too many or too few are being informed.

In the vertical analysis the total load placed on those involved in the project is assessed for each party separately. There must be a discussion about whether it has taken on too much or too little a role in the project. For example, instead of being available just for consultation a party may also be assigned task execution.

TIME SCHEDULING AND RESOURCE ESTIMATION AT GLOBAL LEVEL

In general

Time scheduling is an important aspect of project planning. We have two different situations: 1) the project owner or perhaps others beyond the control of the base organization have determined the completion date; 2) the project will determine the completion date.

An imposed completion date is a situation that a project must accept. There may be several reasons for it, for example:

- The project is based on a strategic decision in the base organization that requires a specific completion date.
- The completion date is based on market considerations. (Because of the market situation the results of the project must be available by a specific date.)

- The project is a sub-project in a larger project. (If the results of the project are not available by a specific date, other projects will be delayed.)
- The completion date is set as a decision by public authorities.
- The results of the project will be used in the organization's annual planning cycle and must be available by a specific date.

Firstly, we will look at the situation where the project determines its completion date. In practice, we find that many projects commit themselves to a specific deadline on grounds that are too loosely defined. Such a point in time has a tendency to become the focal point for those who are monitoring the project. A completion date that is set without adequate knowledge of problems and access to resources becomes a nightmare for the project and damages both morale and results. Essential quality requirements might be set aside in order to finish before the deadline.

We shall illustrate how difficult it is to set a completion date. Consider that a plan shows that a project must go through a series of states. In order to reach a state, a range of activities must be carried out that build upon each other. In PSO projects many activities mean changes for people and the organization that requires maturation, understanding, and support from members of the base organization. In the early stages of a project, the types of activity that must be performed later on are not known in detail. It is therefore very risky to set a 100 per cent binding completion date. It will require large resources to work out an absolutely certain completion date.

Instead, a PSO project focuses on creating a commitment between principal parties to the project and its deliverables. To the best of their abilities, and in recognition of uncertainty, they set an 'anticipated' rather than a 'binding' completion date.

A binding completion date can only be set if all the following conditions are known: all activities to be performed; all the people who will be included in the work; and all extraneous conditions that may affect the project. In order to know all this, most of the work in the project must have actually been completed. A feasibility study (discussed earlier) is one method of obtaining a better basis for estimating the use of time and resources in the project and therefore better anticipates a completion date. But even with such a basis, it is still very difficult to set a binding completion date.

Do not interpret what we have just said as meaning that no time scheduling should be performed. Anticipated completion times for respective milestones should be entered on the milestone plan. At the same time, it must be made very clear that these completion dates are perceived as goals to work towards – not as absolutes to be used later to determine the success of the project.

In general, we have recommended that a project be divided up into phases and sub-projects. The point of such a division is that we concentrate on one part of the project at a time in which it is possible to have insight and in which we can plan with a reasonable degree of certainty. Division into phases makes subsequent time planning more certain.

In order to be able to evaluate and set expected times for completion for the different milestones, we need:

- the milestone plan;
- an activity overview that supplements the milestone plan and shows the most time- and resource-consuming activities;
- the milestone responsibility chart with agreed commitments on resources.

We have gone through the process of drawing up the milestone plan and its milestone responsibility chart. In addition, time scheduling requires that we also prepare an overview of the most time- and resource-consuming activities that must be performed in order to reach the different milestones. The overview does not need to be complete; most important is that it include the activities that demand time and resources.

Time scheduling is performed in connection with the milestone responsibility chart. We take each milestone in turn. The work will be performed in three steps. Firstly, we pinpoint activities that require a great deal of time and resources. Then we estimate the resource requirement for the milestone plan. The resource requirement can be stated in hours, days or weeks of work. Man-days are usually used. Thereafter the calendar time is planned and the work is plotted on the time calendar.

Let us now turn to the situation where a project's completion date is determined by conditions beyond the project's control. Outside forces (public authorities, a special event on a set date, a demanding customer) have determined that the results of the project must be available on a specific day. For example, the May 17th committee (responsible for preparing for the celebration of the Norwegian National Holiday) should be finished with its work by 17 May.

In such cases, it is also relevant to perform the type of planning we have just demonstrated, but a problem may arise. If the imposed completion date really is an absolute requirement, and if it appears that the calculated project completion date is beyond the imposed date, the project faces a serious challenge.

In such cases it is important to hold a thorough and sober discussion about alternatives, either for an increased amount of resources or for a reduced level of scope, so that the project can be implemented within the time limit. Is it possible, perhaps, to find an acceptable combination of a slightly reduced level of scope and a slightly increased amount of resources? The work on each milestone can be re-examined with a view to possible timesaving.

If it is not possible to find a solution that gives a completion date before the deadline, the project owner or the top management of the base organization must deal with the problem. An acceptable solution will then hopefully be found. If not, and if the project still must deliver before the deadline, the project manager must consider seriously whether he is willing to accept the position of project manager and be responsible for a project that is doomed to failure.

Time scheduling for the project 'Excellent physical work environment'

Let us use the project 'Excellent physical work environment' as an example. In Figure 6.6 we have shown the most time- and resource-consuming activities for the different milestones in this project. We can see that at this stage of planning we make certain decisions on how the milestones will be achieved. This is necessary to be able to draw up a time schedule. Among other things it

---

M1 Description of the present situation
- Prepare a questionnaire
- Wait for response
- Process the replies and collate them in a report

M2 Description of desired situation
- Interview line managers
- Prepare a proposal for the desired situation
- Decide on a desired situation

M3 Requirements for change
- Identify the most important requirements for change

M4 Ideas for measures
- Hold a brainstorming session

M5 Consequences of the measures
- Assess whether a measure will contribute towards the desired situation
- Calculate cost estimates for the measures

M6 Action plan
- Select the measures to be included in the plan
- Calculate the measures in a plan
- Develop an action plan in detail

Figure 6.6 Overview of the most time- and resource-consuming activities of the project 'Excellent physical work environment'

is decided to send out a questionnaire to all employees for inputs to the description of the present situation. It is also decided that line managers will be interviewed to provide a basis for drawing up a rough outline of the desired situation. Other measures with different resource and time requirements could have been chosen.

Using the milestone plan (Figure 5.5), the milestone responsibility chart (Figure 6.5) and the rough activity overview (Figure 6.6) as a basis, we can start the scheduling. We look first at the work on the milestone that will end with a description of the present situation.

Estimating the resources requirements for this milestone means assessing the work input required to reach it. We pose the question: If the work is performed in a concentrated manner, without any interruptions, how many days (or hours or weeks) of work will it take? In order to provide such an estimate we must look more closely at the resource-consuming activities involved in reaching the milestone. In this case the major part of the resources will be used in drawing up the questionnaire, processing the replies, and drawing up the report. We know from the responsibility chart that the work will be a cooperative effort involving the project manager, the personnel consultant and the environment committee. The affected line managers must be consulted. The external consultant should provide assistance for training. These are the resources we assess for the work to be executed. We believe that the work will require 10 mandays.

Thereafter, the work towards achieving the milestone should be put into calendar time. How long the work will take, and when it should be performed, depends on the availability of the people being considered and how time-consuming the different activities are. We know that in this case it is necessary to wait for a response to the questionnaire. This is not a resource-consuming activity, but it demands calendar time. Moreover, holidays, illness and other absences, interruptions and breaks in the work, and other tasks that project members will perform must be taken into consideration. We assume that it will take 20 calendar days to reach the milestone.

The time schedule for the milestone will be recorded on a bar chart; see Figure 6.7. The planned time period for working on the milestone will be marked with a horizontal line. The date set for completion can be marked with a vertical line.

We then proceed to the next milestone. We have shown that the work on developing a description of the desired situation will require 15 man-days. The work on this milestone can start before the previous one is reached. Interviews with line managers can be prepared and dates can be agreed upon when there is a rough idea of the employees' picture of the present situation. There is no need to wait until the report is completed. When assessing how long the work on this milestone will take, it is important to take into consideration that it includes a decision-making process. Line managers and the managing director must decide how they want the physical work environment to be. It often takes longer to make these decisions than initially anticipated. It is important to form a clear picture of the time the decision-makers will need to arrive at their conclusions. Work on this milestone is estimated to take one month altogether.

Man-days	Start	Week 2 4 6 8 10 12 14	End	No.	Milestone	Project manager	Managing director	Affected line manager	Personnel consultant	Work environment comm.	External consultant
10	1/1		20/1	M1	Description of present situation	X/P	A	C	X	X	T
15	10/1		10/2	M2	Description of desired situation	X/P	D	d	X	C	
1	10/2		12/2	M3	Requirements for change	X/P			X	I	
5	10/2		1/3	M4	Ideas for measures	X/P		C	X	C	A
5	1/3		20/3	M5	Consequences of the measures	X/P		X	X	I	
10	20/3		10/4	M6	Action plan	X/P		C	X	C	

Figure 6.7 Time schedule for the project 'Excellent physical work environment'

Work on the next milestone follows the same procedure. Any feasibility or follow-up work can be marked with a dotted line on the time schedule. Some preparations for the writing of the action plan will be done at an early stage. This means that principles can be drawn up for the word-processed text, for example, and for the layout of the report. Special events, for example a seminar or, in this case, a brainstorming session, can be marked with an X.

The combination of a responsibility chart and a time schedule provides a good, focused picture of the planned progress of a project. When a schedule has been drawn up on the responsibility chart, the anticipated completion dates for the milestones can be transferred over to the milestone plan. We thus obtain a milestone plan with completion dates for the different milestones.

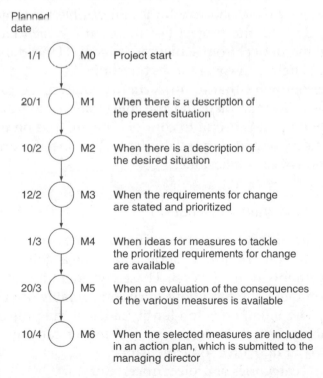

Planned date

1/1 — M0 — Project start

20/1 — M1 — When there is a description of the present situation

10/2 — M2 — When there is a description of the desired situation

12/2 — M3 — When the requirements for change are stated and prioritized

1/3 — M4 — When ideas for measures to tackle the prioritized requirements for change are available

20/3 — M5 — When an evaluation of the consequences of the various measures is available

10/4 — M6 — When the selected measures are included in an action plan, which is submitted to the managing director

Figure 6.8 Milestone plan with completion dates for the project 'Excellent physical work environment'

Figure 6.8 shows the milestone plan with completion dates for the project 'Excellent physical work environment'. We again stress that we are talking about anticipated dates. Setting a binding completion date of the project is not the most important goal of project planning. Project planning should ensure first and foremost that the project works on the right things, and that it has a good basis for achieving the desired end state.

UNCERTAINTIES OF THE PROJECT

It is important to evaluate uncertainties confronting the project. The project has committed itself to create certain results with a certain quality within specific time and resource limits. The commitment is expressed as a milestone plan. The milestone responsibility chart shows who is responsible for achieving the results. But will the project be successful? Which factors may prevent the project from achieving its goals? Uncertainty analysis should help us answer theses questions.

We recommend that an uncertainty analysis be carried out after the milestone plan and the milestone responsibility chart are drawn up. It is useful to conduct the analysis on two levels: 1) a general uncertainty evaluation; 2) a specific uncertainty evaluation of each milestone.

General uncertainty evaluation

In the general part we want to point out some conditions that are particularly important to include when one is going to evaluate the uncertainty of the project. These considerations do not pass off as complete; the conditions vary considerably from project to project. The intention is to identify sides of the project that are particularly uncertain, so the project leader can consider if he wants to put into force some measures.

General categories of project uncertainty:

- environment;
- project plans and project organization;
- conduct of the decision-makers;
- access to resources in the project.

The first element (the environment) takes up the question of how the project may be influenced by external conditions; the second (plans and organization) considers internal conditions of the project, while the two last (decisions and access to resources) are attached to the relationship between the base organization and the project.

Figure 6.9 is a list of factors that are important to discuss when one wants to form a true picture of what uncertainties the project is confronted with in general.

If the completion date is an absolute deadline, the uncertainty evaluation should be as complete as possible.

Firstly, we look at what uncertainties the environment creates for the project. Events can happen that the project has no control over. The uncertain conditions need to be identified and the project needs to establish how it will act in relation to the uncertainty.

We do, of course, try to make as good a plan as possible and organize ourselves as sensibly as possible. A quality evaluation of plans and organization will contribute to ensure quality of the project and the product. We may, for example, still question how certain we feel about implementing the plans we have made. We ask whether the plans are realistic. Projects do tend to start slowly, but many plans are based on high pace from day one. What will happen if we lose pace from the very beginning? What can we do to secure pace from the beginning?

We should further discuss the uncertain ground on which the project operates. The project is a new and unfamiliar task. Using unfamiliar technology represents additional uncertainty. There is also reason to consider the stakeholders' attitude towards the project. Our plan will be much stronger if we make a stakeholder analysis and develop measures to secure support for the project.

During activity planning, we will estimate how long it takes to execute the different activities of the project. Such estimates will always be encumbered with uncertainties. It is quite possible that some people intentionally propose low estimates to get approval of the project. Uncertainty evaluation of estimates is especially important for milestones that demand a high level of resources. This is often where big 'cracks' can be found.

Environment:
- May users (customers, clients, members of the base organization) change their minds in ways that will affect the project?
- May top management of the base organization or line managers change their minds in ways that will affect the project?
- May competitors act in ways that will affect the project?
- May public authorities impose rules or regulations that will affect the project?
- May nature behave in ways that will affect the project?

Project plans and project organization:
- Is the milestone plan based on a realistic view of resource requirements, access to resources and calendar time? Have we drawn up a project plan which may break down unacceptably in total or in specific periods?
- Which parts of the plan are most critical with regard to project progress and to the quality of project deliverables?
- Is the technology one that is new to us?
- Have we managed to describe and scope the project in such a way that it will not grow out of control?
- Can we count on complete loyalty to the plan from the base organization, or will it meet resistance? What is likely to be most controversial?
- Are there milestones that are not clear and which express several intentions rather than one clearly described state? Which milestones does this apply to, and how critical are they?
- Which estimates are most critical in relation to elapsed time? Does a systematic method of approach lie behind the estimates – or is it just a case of 'think of a number'? Are the estimates arrived at through a recommended procedure?

The conduct of the decision-makers:
- Which decisions are most critical in the project? What happens if we do not obtain these decisions in time? What happens if they must be made again? What are the consequences of this for progress and costs?
- Have we allotted a realistic interval from completion of the basis for a decision until a decision is made upon it? Have all the decision-makers checked that they are available during the decision-making period?
- Is the base organization's culture such that we can count on obtaining lasting decisions or are decisions regularly ducked or postponed?

Access to resources in the project:
- Which parts of the project work are the most critical with regard to access to resources?
- Are there certain parts of the base organization which have a habit of never providing the agreed resources at the agreed time?
- Will the project members regard the project as important, or will they downgrade project work in favour of everyday base organization work?
- Are we particularly vulnerable in certain areas if we do not obtain all the required resources?

Figure 6.9 Factors when assessing project uncertainties

Finally, we shall focus on two areas closely connected to the base organization: decision-making and access to resources. Decisions of relevance must be made by members of the base organization, and usually by the line managers. They also need to transfer resources to the project. In the uncertainty evaluation, we ask ourselves how certain we think we are that correct decisions will be made when they are required; and how certain we think we are that the project will get adequate resources at the right time. If we find an unacceptable uncertainty, measures need to be carried out to improve the situation.

Uncertainty in the milestone level

An uncertainty analysis should be performed on each milestone. The following factors should be discussed (these can also be presented in a table, see Figure 6.10):

- uncertainty element (what can occur that will influence the project);
- probability (how big is the probability that it will occur);
- consequence (what is the consequence for the project if it does happen);
- action (what do we do);
- responsibility (who does it).

Firstly, one should identify what might occur to influence the project. One might think in terms of the general uncertainty categories that were discussed above, but it may be easier to think of future events connected to specific milestones. We should identify events that may influence the project in either a negative or positive way.

Milestone	Uncertainty element	Probability	Consequence	Action	Responsible

Figure 6.10 Uncertainty matrix for the milestones of a project

Next, we should consider the probability that a specific condition might occur. It is sufficient to rate the probability as high, medium or low. Then we need to consider the consequence if the condition occurs, using the same ratings. If we wish to look in more detail, we can evaluate sub-elements of the milestone such as completion date, the cost, and the quality.

Uncertainty analysis should result in an action that needs to be initiated, and indicates who is responsible for its implementation.

Uncertainty analysis for the project 'Excellent physical work environment'

Figure 6.11 shows the results of an uncertainty analysis for the first two milestones of the project that work with the development of an action plan to improve the work environment (the milestone plan was presented in Figure 5.5). It is not necessary to do an uncertainty analysis for all the milestones at the beginning of the project. One should wait until work on the actual milestone is about to get started, the best basis for the analysis. The result of the uncertainty analysis is presented in an uncertainty matrix.

The uncertainty matrix shows a condition of uncertainty: excessively negative descriptions of the current physical work

Milestone	Uncertainty element	Probability	Consequence	Action	Responsible
M1 When there is a description of the present situation	Dishonest responses	Small	Large (quality)	Information and motivation	Project manager
	Project members busy with other work	Medium	Large (time)	Agreement with line manager	Project manager
M2 When there is a description of the desired situation	Line managers not available for interviews	Medium	Larger (time)	Managing director asks them to allocate time	Project manager

Figure 6.11 Uncertainty matrix for the first milestones of the project 'Excellent physical work environment'

environment by people in the base organization. The probability for this is low, but the consequence will be high, since the description of the present situation will be the basis for the remainder of the project work. Therefore, the project has decided to implement an information and promotional campaign to explain the purpose of the project and the importance of responding to the survey with accurate descriptions of the present conditions. The project leader has the responsibility. The uncertainty analysis has further identified some other uncertainty elements that demand concrete measures.

7

Detail planning and detail organization

In this chapter, we shall discuss detail planning and detail organization and deal with them together. We shall use the generic term activity planning for these two tasks.

We first present factors that are essential to activity planning. Then we examine the approach for this type of planning. We shall show how the responsibility chart plays a central role in activity planning as well.

PRINCIPLES OF PROJECT ACTIVITY PLANNING

The first principle we emphasize is that the planning and organization of individual activities in a project should not be done before it is strictly necessary. Because of the great emphasis on activity scheduling methods, one often sees detailed plans for activities that are to be performed far in the future, possibly after several months or, worse yet, several years. Much effort expended on this sort of planning is wasted. Before the day arrives when the work was planned to start, changes will have occurred that render the plan useless. Some planned activities may have been eliminated as the project may have taken a course that makes them superfluous. And if they are to be executed, rational planning and organization requires that we know the results of earlier tasks that are the foundation. The people originally planned to do the work may not be available, and therefore the estimates are no longer valid. Information of this type is not usually available until we are relatively close to the starting time for an activity.

The other principle we emphasize is that those who will perform the work must also be included in planning and organizing it. This was also shown in Figure 4.9 (the example of a principle responsibility chart) which illustrated what is generally considered to be a good division of work between the line manager, project manager and implementers. When implementers participate in activity planning, the plans will be better; their involvement further increases their morale and identification with the project. Activity planning may well occur during normal project meetings, in which reports on earlier activities in the project are examined, discussions occur on how to make up any delays, and general problems in the project are addressed.

ACTIVITY PLANNING

Activity planning is the drawing up of a detail plan to achieve the milestones of the milestone plan. It is through activity planning that we determine how to reach the milestones within the time limits and with the resources allocated.

Activity responsibility chart

A major part of activity planning is performed with the help of the activity responsibility chart. Therefore, we will first examine what an activity responsibility chart is.

In the previous chapter, we gave a general description of responsibility charts. We also showed the use of the milestone responsibility chart. It clarifies the role of the different parties necessary to achieve the milestones. The activity responsibility chart is subordinate to the milestone responsibility chart. It identifies specific people who will perform the various activities within the agreed-upon guidelines described in the milestone responsibility chart.

When making an activity responsibility chart we use the activities to be executed as the starting point. Then we decide upon specific people to be assigned to these activities. The milestone responsibility chart shows which parties the people should be drawn from. The chart also describes who will have the right to make decisions or to express opinions.

The activity responsibility chart has one advantage in comparison with a number of other activity planning techniques in that it not only shows who will perform the different activities, but it also brings attention to other important matters, such as decision-making authority, progress responsibility, consultation and information activities.

Making the activity responsibility chart is an important clarification process – just as making the milestone responsibility chart was. Those who will work on the activities must meet, discuss and agree upon what the activity responsibility chart shall look like. Every person who is to have a role in this part of the project must participate in this process and have the opportunity to apply the appropriate symbols to his own name.

When setting up an activity responsibility chart, certain individuals may be assigned too many symbols. Some may take on too many jobs and roles. Here the project manager must be on guard – overloaded project members can have a negative effect on the progress of the project. A 'crossing-off' round is sometimes necessary.

Some people will want to take on jobs for which they have neither the expertise nor the authority. The activity responsibility chart makes it possible to establish the principle that professional decisions should be made by those who are normally responsible for them in the base organization. These are the people who should be allocated the decision-making symbol. And an important point – only those people who actually have a decision-making symbol on the responsibility chart are the ones who should make decisions. There is a strong tendency in projects for everyone to want to join in and discuss everything – including matters for which they are not responsible and do not have expertise. This hinders the project. This type of over-participation can be prevented if the activity responsibility chart is set up properly and followed.

The activity responsibility chart organizes work on the activities in the project. We need to supplement the activity responsibility chart with a time schedule. Estimates for the use of resources must be made and the work on the different activities must be put into calendar time.

The activity responsibility chart does not need to repeat the responsibility for decision-making processes if they are described precisely enough on the milestone responsibility chart. Decision symbols on the activity responsibility chart often stand for quality approval.

Stages in activity planning

Activity plans are made for each milestone individually. We do not start activity planning before it is necessary. The person who is responsible for progress for the milestone (capital letter 'P' on the milestone responsibility chart) and the project manager must decide when the planning work should start. Activity planning can be divided into four stages:

1. Identify all the activities that must be performed to reach the milestone.

For each activity:

2. Identify all the people who will be affected by each activity, and determine how they should be involved in the work.
3. Estimate the work effort necessary for the execution of each activity in a unit of time (eg hours).
4. Estimate the work duration for each activity in calendar time.

Usually, planning takes place during a project meeting where all the affected project members are present.

Stage 1

It is best to draw up an individual activity plan for each milestone. The first stage in the work will thus be to find all the activities that must be completed to reach the milestone. A great deal of help is provided by the work done previously in connection with time scheduling for the milestone plan. This provides a starting point for activity planning but the final list of activities may be completely different from the one developed in connection with the milestone plan.

There are several reasons for this, including:

- The list of activities previously developed wasn't intended to be complete.
- A great deal of guesswork lay behind the initial list.
- The activities already completed in the project have raised the level of knowledge of what should now be done.
- A completely different approach than that originally considered can be chosen.
- The level of ambition may have changed significantly.

The list of activities developed during milestone time scheduling is a good basis for the work to find relevant activities now. Completing the activity plan will be much easier if a model exists to guide the definition of activities. (For example, a systems development model may be of assistance if a computer system is to be developed.)

An activity should fulfil certain requirements:

- It should not require an unduly large work input or effort – a maximum of 80 man-hours or 10 man-days.
- It must be possible to check that the activity has been completed.

Both requirements facilitate control. As an example, perhaps we have an activity that is large in work effort and calendar time. According to our requirements above, it will likely be difficult to control. During execution, reports may show everything going well for a long period of time, and then, as the activity nears completion, problems arise. Upon further analysis, we find that the activity is by no means finished, and a considerable amount of work remains. If activities are smaller as we recommend, problems can be detected much faster.

It is also important to be able to ascertain whether an activity has finished. It may be necessary to define specific criteria to ensure that this is so. Ideally, a person other than the implementer should be able to state whether the activity has been carried out satisfactorily. If criteria have not been defined for an activity's completion or for its standards of quality, it will be very difficult to control.

Stage 2

The people to work on each individual activity must be identified. The milestone responsibility chart will assist us in doing this. It establishes which parties (sub-organizations) should be included in completing the particular milestones. The project owner will already have approved its contents and all involved parties should have also accepted it, therefore they should identify specific people to complete the activities. Their roles should be clarified as well.

Stage 3

After it has been decided who should perform an activity and roles have been established, the effort required to carry out the plan must be estimated. A copy of the responsibility chart may be given to each participant. Individuals estimate their work effort on their own copy. It could be stated in man-hours, -days or -weeks. Next, the estimates are discussed with the project manager. The project manager and the implementer(s) jointly decide on the effort required. As explained previously, it is very important that this be a cooperative effort.

Stage 4

When the amount of work effort required for implementation of the activity is established, we discuss its duration, how it should be laid out in calendar time, and consider its relationship to other activities

The project manager must decide when it is best to carry out the activity; however, the implementer's line manager (who is the person who can commit the use of resources) should also be brought into the discussion. There may be factors in the base organization requiring the activity to be scheduled at another time even when this is not perceived as ideal by the project.

When estimating an activity's calendar duration, the fact that a member can work far less than 100 per cent of his time on the activity must be considered. In addition to the project member's duties, other factors must be considered such as illness, compassionate leave, courses and seminars, etc.

Through scheduling, an understanding is gained about which activities are time critical. These activities will delay the overall project if they are delayed. During the project meeting, it is important to design the allocation of work such that the time-critical activities are the ones over which the project has most control. The responsibility for time-critical activities should not lie with those who have a very heavy workload, either within the project or outside it. In order to avoid this, a further discussion should occur regarding redistributing work and about relieving work responsibilities such that members can focus more on time-critical activities.

Tools in activity planning

We recommend that supportive previous experience and other relevant material be sought during activity planning. At this level of planning, thoroughness and precision are more important than creativity.

Models or templates can be useful tools. It is relatively easy to find activity models for technical problems that describe specific technical activities that must be executed. It can ensure that no activities will be forgotten. It is much more difficult to find a model for PSO projects as there may be no models with a direct connection to this type of problem. For PSO projects a general problem-solving model that describes a process to solve a problem may then be an appropriate model to use.

Activity responsibility chart for the project 'Excellent physical work environment'

Figure 7.1 shows an example of an activity responsibility chart. Our project 'Excellent physical work environment' has now progressed so far that the activities leading up to the first milestone M1, 'When there is a description of the present situation', have been identified. It is now important that the activity list is complete. It is no longer sufficient simply to indicate the most time- and resource-consuming activities as we did in the time scheduling in Figure 6.6.

Man-days	Start	Week 1	Week 2	Week 3	End	No.	Activities	Karyn – Project manager	Alan – Managing director	Mary – Head production	Paul – Head sales	Louise – Head personnel	Barry – Personnel consultant	Rose – Work env. com. tant	Arnold – Consultant
4	1/1	◆			6/1	M1.1	Draw up draft of a questionnaire	X/P					X		
1	8/1		◆		10/1	M1.2	Gather views on the questionnaire	P	A	C	C	C			
1	9/1		◆		11/1	M1.3	Determine final form questionnaire	X/P					X		T
1	1/1	◆	◆		10/1	M1.4	Set up mailing list						X/P		
0,5	12/1		◆		12/1	M1.5	Send out questionnaire						X/P		
0,5	17/1			◆	17/1	M1.6	Send out reminders						X/P		
2	12/1		◆	◆	19/1	M1.7	Process the replies	X/P					X		A
3	16/1			◆	20/1	M1.8	Draw up the report	X/P					X		A

Figure 7.1 Activity responsibility chart with time schedule for the first milestone of the project 'Excellent physical work environment'

8

Project control

WHAT IS CONTROL?

Many people believe that reporting and project control are one and the same thing. This is not so. Reporting is describing what has occurred and what the situation is. Control is doing something about what the reports show.

We must have reports to be able to check whether the project is sticking to the plan. The purpose of reports is not to establish grounds for punishment or reward. The purpose is to establish whether there is a need for corrective measures – while there is still time to take those measures.

Control is management, not paperwork. Control involves analysing the situation, deciding what to do and then doing it. But control presupposes that a certain amount of paperwork (reporting) be done. Control is the crux of project management. Nevertheless, it is often misunderstood by both management and project staff. The reason may be that people have had many negative experiences. They are used to extensive bureaucracy, where reports are sent out left, right and centre, while everyone knows that either no one reads them, or in the worst case they are used to denounce those who are not following the plan.

Control is not the same as persecution. Reports are needed not to find out whether people have been on the job eight hours a day, but to determine whether or not it is necessary to change course. Project management must have the ability to make decisions based on the reports they receive; otherwise all reporting is in vain.

Let us illustrate what control is by looking at decisions that can be made if reporting reveals that there is a lapse in project progress. When it shows that it is not possible to achieve the completion date set for an activity or a milestone, the following possibilities exist:

- move the completion date;
- lower the level of ambition;
- bring in additional resources;
- rearrange the workload.

One may accept the consequences of being delayed by deciding to move the current milestone and affected subsequent milestones. If one does not wish to do this, the deadline can be met if the level of ambition is lowered. This is not always feasible but often it will be possible to do something. One may in addition bring in more, or higher performing resources. Again, we know that it is difficult in practice to achieve great effects through increased resources, but it may be possible to get some benefit. Work can also be redistributed, for example, assigning the most able people to the time-critical activities.

Not everyone believes that it helps to bring additional resources into projects. Brooks coined his law on the basis of his experiences when working on the operating system for the IBM 360 series. It states: 'Adding resources to a late project makes it later.' Brooks had delayed software projects in mind when he formulated this law, but today it is used for all types of projects. The background for it is that when staffing is increased in a project, those who are already working on it have to spend time introducing the new staff to the project and training them. Real work input into the project's activities actually falls.

Our basic point is that there are two attitudes that should not be permitted and cause damage to all project works. They are: 'It will probably be OK' and 'We'll wait and see'.

It is rather bad if a project is off schedule and nobody realizes it before it is too late to do anything about it. But as a rule this is not the main problem. The most common problem is that people know that a plan is off schedule, but they do not have the will or the power to do anything about it. We warn against a 'head-in-the-sand' mentality, where people are not willing to acknowledge problems and initiate the necessary measures.

Below we present certain principles that can strengthen control of project work. We then discuss control measures for activities and milestones.

PRINCIPLES OF PROJECT CONTROL

We will first formulate certain principles that we consider to be fundamental for reporting and control. Thereafter we will show how they can be used in practice.

Reporting – not bureaucratic and tedious

In the majority of cases reporting is tedious. This applies especially when things are going badly. It is not pleasant to report that the project is not running according to plan.

Exception reporting is a much-used reporting principle. It means that only variances from the plan will be reported (and these are mainly negative variances). We are opposed to this. It means that people only communicate when there are problems, and this is not particularly pleasant, either for the person receiving or the one providing the information. A communication imbalance is formed in the organization – a preoccupation with everything that goes wrong. It is very important to bring out what is going according to plan.

Even if everything is going well, however, reporting is often perceived to be bureaucratic and tedious. It is associated with 'desk work' that takes time away from 'real' work. This perception will never be eradicated completely, but it can be minimized. In practice, this means reporting should be reduced to the absolute minimum with regard to control. It also means that a balance must be found between written reporting (that is particularly tedious) and conversations and group discussions that elaborate on matters raised in the report wherever necessary.

Something that creates a particular distaste for reporting is the feeling that the whole reporting process is worthless because it is done as a matter of habit rather than as a basis for action. It is done because it is an accepted required procedure, but without enthusiasm and without any belief that it will improve the work situation for oneself or for the project.

Many people have filled in large report forms, seen them collected, sorted, and then put in a file on a shelf. The project manager is often unwilling to go into issues discussed in the report. The most that comes of these issues is that he will 'make a note of them'. Project members know that the only thing the project manager is concerned about is that everyone has submitted his report.

This attitude can be changed if project members feel that control is actually taking place. It must happen through discussions and analysis that result in measures that improve the situation for the project. Then reporting will be experienced as being useful and motivating.

Defined control criteria

Effective control requires that one decides in advance which matters must be kept under special review during the project. Matters to be reported on and discussed must have been identified when control measures were established. If project members are allowed to report on what they consider to be most important, haphazard reporting will result. Clearly defined control criteria should exist and be built into the report form.

We should not allow reporting from project members to depend too much on free text. The result tends to be very short messages ('OK') or long accounts of trivialities. There is a danger the report will reflect the immediate energy level of the report writer (which can be low on a Friday afternoon) or his linguistic ability to camouflage the real state of affairs.

We recommend that one focuses instead on some previously defined conditions. It is important to make reporting so simple that the words 'Yes' and 'No' are sufficient. If it is necessary to elaborate further on matters, then do so in a conversation. Conversations held as reporting and control elaborations must be structured. Many conversations between the project manager and project members are not really goal directed and mostly take the form of 'cosy chats'. The project manager perches on the edge of the member's desk and asks, 'How's it going?' The conversation ranges back and forth over more or less chance matters in the project.

The report form should, as mentioned, focus on previously defined control criteria. It is just as important that any supplementary conversations also have the same focus. Conversations must be directed towards discovering the causes of any deficiencies and identifying action to put the project back on course.

We also stress that it is important that the reporting and control discussions occur between the people who are responsible for these tasks, as shown by the principle responsibility chart. In practice we often see that status reports and discussions occur at project meetings where some people present have little or no connection with the matter at hand. The presence of these people hampers the openness necessary for discussion of an unpleasant situation and the possible choice of unpopular measures. They rarely have anything to contribute to the discussion and in the best case only serve to prolong it.

Reporting on the plan

An important principle is that reporting should occur on a document that also shows the actual plan. Each time a report is made, it must subsequently be compared with the plan. This ensures that one keeps to the point. Other reporting methods should not be permitted. In order to simplify reporting, the plan document should have room to accommodate reporting. When the plan is finalized, sufficient copies should be prepared for use during all subsequent reporting.

Reporting on the plan document also has the advantage of easily ensuring that the right people receive reports and follow up. It is important to send a report that shows a deviation from the plan to the person who has the authority to do something about it or one who can take steps to get the project back on course again.

Reporting according to a predetermined pattern

All reporting should be done according to a set pattern. This often means that reports will be given at fixed intervals. Discipline is necessary otherwise it is easy for reporting to be neglected.

The frequency of reporting depends on the level. Reports can be less frequent at the milestone level than at the detail level because of the longer time horizon. It is more important that variances be detected quickly at detail level so that corrective measures can be introduced before these variances have gone on too long.

In general, at the milestone plan level, we recommend monthly reporting and control. Alternatively, we can do the reporting when each milestone is scheduled to be reached. At the activity level the frequency of reporting must be agreed upon internally within the project. Usually reporting every week or every two weeks is appropriate.

CONTROLLING ACTIVITIES

We will begin by discussing control of activities. It is natural to start our discussion here as what is going on at this level governs what must be done at the milestone level.

Criteria for controlling activities

At the detail level we plan the activities necessary to achieve the milestones. Activity plans are drawn up and documented on the activity responsibility chart. In accordance with the control principles, reporting will occur on the plan document (Chapter 11 introduces the form to be used to document the activity responsibility chart). We will ask for reporting on seven different matters:

1. use of resources;
2. time schedule;
3. quality;
4. responsibility chart;
5. changes/additions;
6. waiting time;
7. special problems.

1. Use of resources

The use of resources in the project is obviously one of the matters that must be monitored. It is important to ascertain whether one has used, or will use, the resources stated in the plan. We recommend reports on:

- actual resources used to the present (work done);
- outstanding requirement for resources (work to do);
- total use of resources (sum = work done + work to do).

The simple summary can be compared with the estimate to monitor the overall usage of resources. Our experience is that it is easier to get a project member to give a good estimate of the outstanding requirement than to ask him to give a percentage estimate of the completion status. When asked for a percentage figure, it is tempting to say that the activity is 90 per cent complete even if it hasn't progressed nearly so far.

2. Time schedule

The question of whether the project is on schedule, ie whether the activity will be completed on time, is also important. The plan shows when the activity should be completed. In a report we could pose the question: Completed on time? The question must be answered Yes or No. As an alternative we could ask for the completion date.

3. Quality

Over the past few years there has been increased attention to the importance of quality. It is important to be sure that this philosophy also reigns in project work.

One of the most frequent causes of delays in projects is that the quality of the work is not good enough. Work may have been executed inaccurately or incompletely such that rework is necessary. Therefore, this is the basis for asking for a report on whether the quality is approved. Quality approval can be agreed upon, but is often one of the things that is neglected in practice. Therefore the question: Is quality accepted? must be answered Yes or No.

4. Responsibility chart

The activity responsibility chart defines precisely who should perform the various roles in connection with an activity. Experience has shown that there can be problems releasing the necessary people from their daily jobs in the base organization.

In projects it can also be difficult to achieve the necessary decisions. Therefore, it is important to have a report on whether the work pattern described by the responsibility chart is being followed, or whether there are variances. We ask: Is the responsibility chart kept? The question must be answered Yes or No.

5. Changes/additions

It is important to ascertain whether the original plan is being used as the basis to monitor the work. Often when starting work on an activity, new information makes it obvious that things should be done differently. When evaluating resource usage and project progress, one needs to know whether the work was done according to the original plan, or whether changes or additions were made. Therefore the question: Changes/additions? must be answered Yes or No.

6. Waiting time

A project works with limited resources. Therefore, it is important to use the available resources in the best possible way. Someone sitting around waiting for inputs to their activity is a waste of resources and should be addressed. Therefore, we ask the question: Waiting time? The question must be answered Yes or No.

7. Special problems

It is also desirable to know whether there have been any special problems encountered while conducting the activity work. It is not easy for a project manager to detect all problems. Therefore, the report writer needs to indicate whether he has experienced any difficulties. He is asked the question: Special problems? It must be answered Yes or No.

In addition to 'Yes or No' answers, reports should offer an opportunity to elaborate on what seems to be the central problem in the project. One is given an opportunity to specify:

- problem description;
- cause: why the problem has arisen;
- consequence: what the consequences of the problem are for the project;
- suggested action: what can be done about the problem.

The activity report writer should indicate whether the variances from the plan or the problems the project is experiencing are so serious that they may impact the milestone level. He should state if his progress has any consequences for the milestone plan. This means that a project member should look at his own work and reflect on the impacts to his team members' work. This will give him a valuable perspective on his activities and on the problems the project may experience.

Good reporting is a challenge. As a minimum, we recommend some questions that can be answered simply with a yes or no, and some regarding actual and anticipated use of resources. This type of reporting is not very onerous, yet provides the person responsible with control and a good basis for further work. Remember, reports only provide a starting point for control. Where a closer examination of problems is required, further dialogue between the project manager and team members must happen to respond to the situations.

Report dialogue

The report should provide an opportunity for a deeper discussion between the project manager and the team. This is especially true if the use of resources is expected to deviate from those estimated, or if one or more unsatisfactory answers are discovered on the report. A discussion about the project situation motivates better reporting and improves the project environment. It shows that reporting and control are taken seriously.

The discussion should start by acknowledging that the plan has gone off course, but not irreversibly. It is much worse if the project manager does not realize the problematic situation in time. The plan must not be perceived as fixed in stone. The members must not be so afraid of variances that they do not dare report them. But neither should members just add 10 per cent if the plan is in trouble. The plan should be viewed as being realistic and binding. Vigorous efforts should be made to discover what is going wrong.

Discussions between the project manager and project members must therefore be goal directed. They must be clearly structured with regard to discovering the real causes for any deviation between the plan and the actual situation. We will discuss some factors that are important when discussing different headings in the report.

1. Use of resources

If a resource estimate appears to be wrong, it is important to clarify whether this is a one-time error, or whether we are facing a systematic estimation error. Particularly when several similar examples of variance are discovered, it may lead us to believe there has been widespread miscalculation. The consequence of this should be that the estimation methods should be re-examined and all the estimates re-evaluated.

Often, one cause of inaccurate resource estimates is that a project member's proficiency is overrated and he is asked to do work for which he is not qualified. Plans and estimates must be drawn up based on the people available – they must not be based on brilliant people who do not exist. If project members do not have the necessary knowledge at the outset, time for training must be built into the plans at the start.

2. Time schedule

The estimated resource need for an activity cannot be fulfilled but yet the time schedule can still be met; this means that slack was built into the schedule. Again, it is important to discuss whether this is unique to the current situation, or if it was a general way of doing scheduling. If one was generous when making the schedule, the project manager might assume that there is some leeway in the outstanding activities.

For projects in which time is the most critical success factor, we recommend avoiding the 'student paper' syndrome. We all may recall a paper we were assigned to write that was due at the end of a school course. Many of us can also recall deferring work on writing that paper until the last days of the course, which put us in danger of not completing it within the scheduled time and required us to work extreme overtime to complete it. Unfortunately, it seems to be human nature for many of us to use all the time that is scheduled. Therefore, if slack exists in all activities, the overall project schedule will be much longer than necessary.

Activity estimates are quite often '100 per cent estimates' that include slack to guarantee finishing in 100 per cent of its schedule time. When all activities are then scheduled, the effect is an overall schedule that is much longer than necessary. We recommend that all activity estimates be '50 per cent estimates' such that there is a 50 per cent probability of an activity taking less time, and 50 per cent probability that it will take more time. In exchange for removing slack from individual activities, we add one appropriately sized 'buffer activity' at the end of the activity chain to provide us slack for the overall schedule. This reduces the effects of the student paper syndrome, and makes managing slack a team responsibility versus an individual responsibility.

If the time schedule cannot be met, it is important first to clarify the implications of this for the project. If the activity that has been delayed is a critical activity, the whole project will be delayed unless measures are taken to make up for the lost time.

If the time schedule breaks down and it cannot be traced back to inadequate resource estimates, it is important to find the cause of the problem. There may be several other reasons for the problem. Here are some typical causes:

- Unforeseen interruption in the work. Examples are illness, compassionate leave, and strikes. These are matters that cannot be anticipated.
- Personnel are not released from the base organization to participate in the project as planned. This means that line management may not have arranged cover for the project members so they could participate to the extent planned.
- Deliberate downgrading of the priority of the project on the part of the line management. Matters may have arisen in the base organization that justify this. Resources will then not be supplied to the project at the rate scheduled during planning.
- Lower priority on the part of the project members. In such cases project members have the time to participate in the project work as planned, but they continue working in the base organization. They may do this because the project work is not motivating to them or because they feel incompetent.
- Poor project management. Cover plans exist, and the project members are willing to participate, but project members may not be informed as to when they should participate.

This list illustrates that these typical problems require completely different solutions. Without knowing the actual causes for getting off schedule it is not possible to work out the right corrective measures. In the case of deliberate downgrading by management, we simply have to accept it and revise plans accordingly. But in the cases of lack of release plans or poor motivation, the project manager can do something.

In the matrix in Figure 8.1 we have shown certain combinations of possible answers to questions on whether the resource estimates and the schedule still hold. The matrix points out what it is particularly important to discuss.

		Time schedule accurate?	
		Yes	No
Work-content estimate accurate?	Yes	No action	Analyse – scheduling methods – cause of delay
	No	Analyse – estimating methods – cause of inaccuracy	Analyse – all four factors

Figure 8.1 Analysing the accuracy of work content estimates and time schedules

3. Quality

We stressed earlier the importance of the quality of what is being produced. On the reporting form we ask whether quality has been approved. Our experience is that one of the most important grounds for failure to complete the whole project within time and budget is that the work on earlier activities does not fulfil quality requirements. This has serious repercussions. Therefore, quality must be regarded as just as important as keeping to schedule and everyone in the project must accept that quality will be evaluated. Responsibility for quality control can be decided through the principle responsibility chart and be put into concrete specific terms on the activity responsibility chart.

Quality control presupposes that people have agreed on what quality is and that the criteria for assessing the result have been decided. This is difficult, especially with PSO projects. In many cases the best method of ensuring quality is to select methods that one knows through experience will give good results. We will discuss quality issues in more detail in the next chapter (Chapter 9).

4. Responsibility chart

On the reporting form one is asked whether the responsibility chart has been followed. For an ordinary project member it is the activity responsibility chart that is most relevant, and his answer will probably be based on it.

A 'No' to the question must be followed up with a more detailed discussion of the responsibility chart. The most common problem is that project members from the base organization are not released to the extent required by the plan, but other problems may also exist.

5. Changes/additions

The report should tell of any changes/additions that have been made in relation to the plan. Planning that occurs a relatively short time before activities are to be performed usually requires fewer changes/additions than planning that occurs a long time in advance. In either case, changes may occur. The most important reasons are:

- Changes occur in some of the underlying assumptions that the project is based upon. These changes may be externally generated (the authorities have passed new regulations which affect whatever is to be done) or come from the base organization (management may have issued new guidelines).
- There is a flaw in the specifications of what the project should achieve. Detail work may reveal that there are flaws or omissions in the specifications upon which the project was based.
- 'Eating whets the appetite.' It is very common for the scope of work to expand beyond what was originally foreseen. If the work is progressing well, people can become more and more ambitious and unconsciously take on more.

We must deal with changes, but they also must be controllable. Uncontrolled changes are one of the common causes of project 'breakdown'. We simply have to accept certain changes (changes from outside or from the project owner), but it is important for the team and the organization to examine the consequences and revise plans.

Other types of changes must be subject to evaluation. Many good ideas crop up along the way in a project; they should not be accepted without being assessed for impacts. A formalized change procedure is necessary in a project. In order to be able to control a project it is important to have an overview of changes that occur.

6. Waiting time

Good utilization of available resources in a project is important. It is sometimes necessary to transfer resources from one activity to another. If used appropriately, good activity scheduling programmes can help us determine which activities are time critical and what can be gained by transferring resources from one activity to another.

The project manager must perform this type of assessment, but again, it is very important that he involves the project members in such discussions.

Activity report for the project 'Excellent physical work environment'

In following this project case, we note that the project officially started per plan as the New Year started, 1 January, but the work did not start until 4 January. The decision to do activity reporting every week should be shown clearly to all project participants on the principle responsibility chart (or other project documents). The first report is dated 10 January. The individual people responsible for the specific activities give reports to the project manager who aggregates all reports into a weekly activity report. During the first week, work has been done on four activities. The project manager himself has been in charge of these activities.

The activity report for the first week is shown as Figure 8.2. We see that a delay has already appeared regarding the second activity. The delay has impacted the third activity. Responses to the questionnaire have not come in as planned. The line managers of the base organization have not responded, as they should have according to the responsibility chart. The project manager has decided to keep to the responsibility chart and wait for their responses, but this has consequences for the time schedule.

CONTROLLING MILESTONES

Correlation between control at activity and milestone levels

We have seen how reporting at the activity level should be performed. The project members report using the form on which the activity plan (activity responsibility chart and time schedule) is described. The report shows clearly whether the plan is being followed. Discussions between the project manager and the project members elaborate on the causes of any discrepancy between the plan and the actual situation.

The project members also know the milestone plan. In their reports they will state whether unwanted developments at the activity level have implications for the milestone plan.

The milestone plan is the project's global plan. It is the project manager's responsibility to report on how the project is developing in relation to the milestone plan. The report is usually sent to the project owner (for example, the managing director or a line manager) or to a steering committee. Others also receive the report for information purposes. The principle responsibility chart shows who shall receive the milestone reports.

It is the project manager's responsibility to follow up the activity reports from the project members. This means that the project manager must introduce corrective measures where needed. In certain cases it is apparent that the plan can no longer be adhered to and a revised plan must be developed. Even if project members have stated that the situation at activity level may negatively impact the milestone plan, the project manager may initiate adequate measures to correct the situation, thereby avoiding changes to the milestone plan. This is one of the big advantages of layered planning and control.

Report date: Project manager
Report by: 10/1

Work done (man days)	Work to do (man days)	Completed on time?	Is quality accepted?	Responsibility chart kept?	Changes required?	Waiting time?	Special problems?
4	0	Y	N	Y	N	N	N
0	1	N	N	Y	N	Y	Y
0	1	N	N	Y	N	Y	Y
1	0	Y	N	Y	N	N	N

Figure 8.2 Activity report for the first activities of the project 'Excellent physical work environment'

Man-days	Start	Week 1	Week 2	Week 3	End	No.	Activities	Karyn – Project manager	Alan – Managing director	Mary – Head production	Paul – Head sales	Louise – Head personnel	Barry – Personnel consultant	Rose – Work env. com.	Arnold – Consultant
4	1/1	◆–◆			6/1	M1.1	Draw up draft of a questionnaire	X/P					X		
1	8/1		◆–◆		10/1	M1.2	Gather views on the questionnaire	P	A	C	C	C			
1	9/1		◆–◆		11/1	M1.3	Determine final form questionnaire	X/P					X		T
1	1/1	◆–◆			10/1	M1.4	Set up mailing list						X/P		
0,5	12/1		◆		12/1	M1.5	Send out questionnaire						X/P		
0,5	17/1			◆	17/1	M1.6	Send out reminders						X/P		
2	12/1		◆–◆		19/1	M1.7	Process the replies	X/P					X		A
3	16/1			◆–◆	20/1	M1.8	Draw up the report	X/P					X		A

Figure 8.2 *continued*

Criteria for controlling milestones

The project manager reports on the milestone plan. The report consists of two parts: 1) the milestones and their mutual dependencies; 2) the expected milestone completion dates. Reporting must cover both of these aspects.

1. The milestones

Milestones play a central role in project management. They express important states through which the project should pass. In a number of cases they also represent important results and have an intrinsic value beyond that of being checkpoints.

Reporting must give an account of which milestones have been reached. It should also state whether anything in particular has occurred in the work towards reaching the milestones that is of interest to the project owner and the steering committee.

2. Completion dates

We have discussed earlier the meaning of the milestone completion dates and the final date of the project and we have stated before that there are other factors of equal importance. We have tried to tone down the focus on dates, but this does not mean in any way that the set completion dates are unimportant. The project manager must regard them as goals and realize that the project will be assessed on whether or not it manages to stay on schedule.

It is therefore important to follow closely the completion dates at the milestone level. Any variance from the anticipated completion date for a milestone must be reported. Equally important as reporting the variance is clarifying the causes for its occurrence.

Report dialogue

In principle, reports should be made on a form that also shows the plan. Obviously this also applies to milestone reports and there is room for this on the milestone form.

Reporting here is less structured than at the activity level. To a great extent, the project manager determines what to report. We assume that he has the ability to analyse the project situation and report the central issues. It is usual to mention the completion of important activities on the milestone plan.

The project manager must always report whether the completion dates for milestones are being adhered to. There is little room for an analysis of the problems on the form, so this must be done in a separate note when necessary. It may be unwise to circulate such an analysis to everyone interested in the progress of the project because it may contain evaluations that have personal or organizational implications.

The milestone report should be a concise account from the project manager to the project owner, steering committee and key people in the base organization. The idea is not that they should have a great deal to read but that they should be able to see at a glance where the project stands. If there are serious problems, they require elaboration in the form of memos and discussions.

If progress has slowed down in relation to the milestone plan, it may be because the conditions agreed upon in the milestone responsibility chart have not been adhered to. It may indeed be that the line management or other members of the base organization are not supporting the project as agreed. If the responsibility chart is not followed, and it has implications for project progress, it is important that this be reported. The project owner or top management of the base organization must be given an opportunity to decide on measures so that the responsibility chart will be followed (or possibly changed). An analysis from the project manager should always conclude with a proposal for action, which the project owner or steering committee can decide upon. Control is finding the actual causes for the deviation and proposing measures to do something about it.

Milestone report for the project 'Excellent physical work environment'

Looking again at the project 'Excellent physical work environment', it has been decided and shown on the principle responsibility chart that milestone reports should be made each time a milestone is planned for completion. This means that the first milestone report should be submitted on 20 January, which is the planned date for milestone M1. The reporting is done on the milestone plan. The project manager is responsible for making the report based on information from the activity reports. The report is sent to the project owner (in this case the managing director).

The milestone report of 20 January is shown as Figure 8.3. It shows that the project is delayed a few days, but the project manager is saying that he assumes that the project will be on schedule for the next milestone. By that he is saying that he does not see the need for any actions from the project owner.

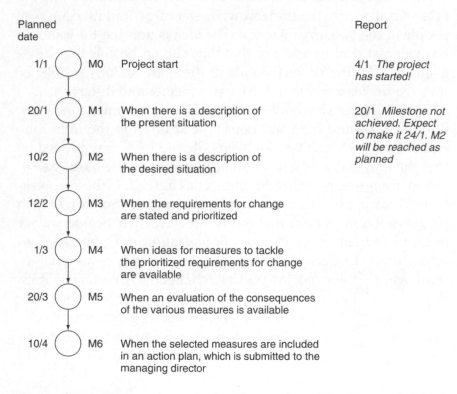

Figure 8.3 Milestone report for the project 'Excellent physical work environment'

9

Quality in project work

In this chapter we will look at what can be done to assure project quality. We discuss the significance of project quality and propose procedures and checklists to secure it.

SIGNIFICANCE OF PROJECT QUALITY

Why is quality important in project work? A silly question perhaps, but it is always important to know what you wish to achieve before starting to take action.

We want quality in project work because it has benefits for the entire base organization; high quality in project work improves the organization. We can distinguish between two categories of projects that affect quality in organizations in different ways:

- Projects where the results change operations internal to the base organization; this means that the quality of the project has direct consequences for the quality of the base organization.
- Projects where the results are delivered to an external organization and the quality of the results determines whether or not the base organization has fulfilled its terms of delivery; this means that the quality has significance for the base organization's reputation and provides opportunities for future contracts.

The first type of project is a typical PSO project. It is intended to create change in the base organization; it should improve it. The project raises the quality of the base organization. The better the quality of the project, the more the quality of the organization is improved.

For such projects there are stringent requirements to be precise in describing what the project is to achieve and to be certain that it can be achieved. Project management must thus facilitate a thorough discussion of the project purpose. It must also manage the interaction between the base organization and the project, because the results will be created in the base organization.

When the project is intended to improve operational quality in the base organization, it must state in concrete terms what it plans to achieve, and how the operation will be changed. The mission breakdown structure (Chapter 4) is a systematic method to obtain an overview of what the project will tackle. It is an important tool in project quality assurance.

PSO projects usually do not create a physical product. It is therefore more difficult to monitor progress than projects where something physical gradually develops, such as bridges, roads or factories. In PSO projects, documents that indicate the project's achievements in all areas under development must be presented at agreed times. Project results must be constantly evaluated in order to ascertain whether the project is on the right course. This is an important part of quality assurance.

Certain organizations create results for other companies through projects. Examples are consultancy firms, research and development organizations, construction companies and IT companies that supply 'tailor-made' products. Quality in project management for these organizations is absolutely essential for their ability to survive. If they do not deliver the results as agreed, their reputation in the market will be seriously damaged. Their projects differ from internal development projects because at the outset there is often a previously defined requirement specification. Therefore their project management methods need not focus so much on identifying project needs. It is more important to be sure that the project satisfies the requirements and specifications while adhering to schedules and budgets.

However, these organizations are increasingly being requested also to supply services to determine the project purpose and implement the desired plan in the customer organization.

Therefore, their emphasis on project management is increasing as well on the accurate and complete definition of project purpose.

PROCEDURES TO INCREASE QUALITY

In order to achieve high quality in project work, it is necessary to introduce standardized procedures. We will not go into the details of procedures, but we will show examples to illustrate their purpose in areas where it is important to establish them.

The contents of the quality assurance procedures depends on whether they are drawn up for internal development projects or for customer supply projects. In the latter case, there are extended requirements in certain areas, such as entering into and complying with contracts. In practice, each organization, that uses the project approach must develop and document its own procedures.

We shall differentiate between two classes of procedures: procedures that are linked to specific phases in a project; and fixed periodic procedures, usually monthly.

The following are examples of areas in which procedures are required.

To prioritize internal development projects

This procedure must be performed once a year and perhaps more frequently if substantial new factors appear. The purpose is to prioritize projects and to plan which projects should be started rather than ad hoc project starts. The procedure presupposes that the organization has mapped its own resource situation, so that it knows what it has available for development objectives. By prioritizing and maintaining an overview of the resource situation, management maintains a current picture as a basis to respond if project efforts must be reduced, or new more important development needs arise.

To formulate purpose and goals and draw up the project mandate

This procedure must be performed early in the project. It is repeated when the situation dictates, for example when there are essential changes in conditions. A complete, regularly updated project mandate ensures that the project focuses on the right things.

To divide the project into phases, sub-projects, etc

This procedure is performed early in the project. The purpose is to provide a foundation for better planning. The procedure ensures that plans are made within reasonable planning horizons. While dividing the project, goals for each section (phase or sub-project) must be described and the resource requirement roughly estimated.

To start each project phase by drawing up milestone plan and milestone responsibility chart

This procedure is performed at the start of each project part or phase. The purpose is for all core project members to acquire a common understanding of the goals and how this part of the project shall progress. This is essential to gain commitment from them. Moreover, people should agree on which milestones are especially critical to the project so that everyone understands the serious consequences if these milestones are not reached in time or are realized with poor quality.

To conclude each project phase with an evaluation

This procedure is performed at the conclusion of each project part or phase. The purpose is to evaluate the results achieved against the milestones, the actual versus planned usage of resources, and how implementation of the responsibility chart went. A summary of changes, additions and obstacles should be developed. Capturing this kind of experience will be useful in the project and contribute to ensuring quality in the long run.

This evaluation procedure can also be performed periodically, not only at the end of a project part or phase. This often provides the team with insights they can use in future work.

To conclude the whole project with an evaluation

This procedure is carried out at the end of the project. The purpose is to analyse systematically the final results of the project in relation to the project's stated purpose and goals. It is also to study which factors contributed positively or negatively to the achievement of purpose and goals. The results of this analysis should be available for future projects, project managers, project owners and project participants.

To hold monthly project meetings

This procedure is performed at least once a month, but usually more often. The purpose is for all current project members to report, agree on responses to make up any delays, plan activities to accomplish the next milestones, hold discussions on professional matters, and discuss specific quality requirements. Each member should report on his own activities and efforts. Each team member must be sure to obtain renewed acceptance for his input into the project from his project manager and line manager.

To obtain acceptance in the steering committee for progress and action

This procedure is performed a short time after a project meeting. The purpose is to obtain acceptance for what has been agreed upon at the project meeting concerning project progress and proposals for actions that will affect progress.

QUALITY OF PLANNING DOCUMENTS

From the base organization's point of view it is essential that planning documents be accurate and usable. Poor plans lead to failing interest in the planning documents as instruments for management. Good plans are necessary if problems in reporting are to be avoided.

If defects in the plans are discovered after the work has started it is too late as the damage has been done and time has elapsed. To avoid this, we recommend that plans should be subject to quality assurance before they are approved.

Quality assurance can take place in several ways. One or more competent individuals can go through the plans together with the project manager. Or the plans can be circulated for comment so that the participants are given an opportunity to offer their opinions of them.

Under no circumstances must the project manager assume a defensive attitude. A difficult situation arises if there is a fundamental flaw in the plan and the project manager is not willing to recognize it. A common answer from the project manager in such cases is: 'This is the best that can be done' or 'You do not understand the situation – the project owner wants a simple plan, not your sophisticated affair.'

This type of reaction arises when we are working on improving quality. We should have a policy established in advance that outlines how we will deal with a situation if someone feels that the plans are inadequate. It may take time to draw up a better plan – but it is possible.

We have developed a checklist for use in quality assurance of plan documents. It is shown in Figure 9.1.

The mandate

- Does the project have a good name, which makes people immediately aware of what the purpose of the project is?
- If the project is given an acronym, does it give people an understanding of what the purpose of the project is?
- Does the mandate clearly state who the project owner is?
- Does the mandate explain the background of the project and its relationships to former projects and works? Is a stakeholder analysis performed so that all stakeholders and their interests are known?
- Is the purpose of the project clearly stated? Is the purpose expressed as a future desired situation for the base organization or for the organization that will make use of the deliverables of the project?
- Are the goals of the project clearly stated? Have we avoided expressing the goals as activities? Are the goals expressed in such a way that a question on whether they are accomplished or not can be answered by Yes or No?
- Is the scope of the project clearly stated? Is a mission breakdown structure presented to make it clear what is inside and outside of the scope of the project?
- Are all limitations to the project work, especially time, costs and quality, determined and clearly stated?
- Has an economic analysis of the project been performed and shown its profitability? Has it been ensured that the project creates something of worth for the base organization?

The milestone plan

- Instead of the present milestone plan, should there be several milestone plans? Does the milestone plan focus on an area of work which is natural to plan as a whole? Does the plan have the proper concentration when it comes to the use of time and resources?
- Is the milestone plan a global plan or does it cover aspects that belong to the activity plans? Is the plan correctly balanced, ie is the degree of detail the same throughout the whole plan?

- Does the milestone plan have a clear structure, correct sequence of milestones, correct logical dependencies between milestones and clear layout?
- Do the result paths reflect what we want to achieve from the project by work? Are the result paths the important professional focus areas of the project?
- Does the milestone plan facilitate parallel progress? Have we avoided a plan that is a 'relay', ie a sequence where all tasks follow one after the other?
- Is the completion date acceptable?
- Will all stakeholders of the project understand the milestone plan?

The individual milestone
- Is the description of the milestone such that it is intelligible outside the project group, ie for affected line managers and others in the base organization?
- Is quality assurance built into the description of the milestone?
- Is approval of quality specified in the description of the milestone?
- Are there references to methods that can ensure quality?
- Can we ascertain whether the milestone has been reached?
- For plans and milestones where creativity is important: Is the description of the milestone neutral as to the solution?
- Are quantitative goals built into the description of the milestone where possible?

The responsibility charts
- Does the division of responsibilities reflect what is possible in the real world, or is it based on wishful thinking?
- Are there more parties/bodies and responsibilities than can be dealt with? In other words, will progress suffer if the responsibility chart is followed?
- Is the division of roles such that quality will be ensured?
- Are important external relationships recognized?
- Have planned absences and possible illness been taken into consideration?
- Have interruptions and other work tasks been taken into consideration when the tasks have been put into calendar time?
- Are any of the resources unrealistically hard pressed?
- Has the fact that decision-making processes take time been taken into consideration? Does the plan ensure that important decisions are made?

Figure 9.1 Checklist for quality assurance of documents in project work

10

Project culture

By project culture we mean the base organization's attitude towards projects and its understanding of project work. In this chapter we shall look at what characterizes a good project culture, and what can be done in general to improve it. We look at the role of the different actors in creating a good project culture. We look at how top management, line management, project owner, steering committee, project management and elected employee representatives should work together for a more successful project environment.

A GOOD PROJECT CULTURE

The project approach is becoming more and more important. This applies to both the public and private sectors. Both government authorities and the business community are constantly facing new demands for change that requires development and improvement. Nowadays problems are complex and are rarely of such a nature that they can be resolved at one specific place in the base organization. Many sections of the organization must be involved. Change and development are complicated and include concepts unfamiliar to many line managers. All-round expertise is required. At the same time, problems must be resolved within a relatively short time span if the organization is not to be weakened competitively or criticized by the public.

The most effective way to meet these challenges is to use the project work form. The ability to use this approach will be significant for the ability of an organization to readjust, develop, and improve itself. The quality of public operations and the survival of companies will depend on how well they will manage their projects.

For good projects, a good project culture is necessary. Project results should be delivered at the agreed time, with the agreed quality and within the agreed use of resources. Ideally, all projects should 'go like clockwork'. It should be possible to take a holiday with a clear conscience – with no project problems looming on the horizon. This imposes demands on the whole organization. This is not only a matter for the project manager and project members. Successful projects are dependent on support from all sectors of the organization. Hence, the importance of project culture. The characteristics of a good project culture are shown in Figure 10.1.

Good project culture must permeate the whole system. Projects have a wide range, and everyone in an organization is important for projects. Even if there is only one line manager or a few members of the base organization who do not pull in the same direction or do not accept the project approach, it can have a severely damaging effect on projects.

A good project culture does not come about by itself. It is necessary to have a special development programme over a long period of time in order to achieve good results. Such programmes often begin by examining the project culture at the outset. We then see what is particularly important to develop further in order to improve attitudes and skills.

A good project culture implies that:
- Everyone in the organization understands the project approach and what it requires by way of interaction between the base organization and the project
- Every project has good and binding plans, at both global (milestone) and detail (activity) levels
- Plans are controlled, so that everyone knows that variances are taken seriously
- The project receives resources from the base organization as agreed upon
- Decisions regarding professional matters are of the quality and within the deadlines agreed upon and to which the base organization has committed itself

Figure 10.1 The good project culture

In this book, we are especially preoccupied with PSO projects and projects where project work is integrated into the base organization. Project culture is particularly important for these types of projects, but it is also significant for other projects, which at first glance do not appear to have the distinguishing features of a PSO project.

Large projects, for example oil exploration in the North Sea and the Winter Olympic Games at Lillehammer, are organized as separate organizations without a need to draw on resources from another base organization. Conflicts between the 'base organization' and the 'project' are not encountered in this type of project. But even within these large projects (perhaps more appropriately categorized as programmes) there are individual projects that have the same characteristics and requirements as those with which we have been particularly concerned.

Certain organizations, construction companies for example, do work for others and use the project work form. They develop a product, which is delivered to the sponsor of the project. It can be a purely technical product – a stretch of road or a bridge, for example. In this case, there is less need for cooperation between the sponsor organization and the contractor's project organization. The contractor will execute the project task on the basis of technical specifications and will supply the completed product. But if the contractor is to supply a more comprehensive solution to a problem that requires needs identification and development within the sponsor's organization, there must be far more cooperation in order for the expected benefits to be achieved.

We have a corresponding situation in the use of subcontractors. The subcontractor's task may be to supply a specified product, but the task may be broadened such that he has to perform development work. This will demand a closer cooperation between the two organizations. The subcontractor's organization then has a great need for cooperation with the sponsor's personnel.

A research and development project may require cooperation for long periods among a small group of researchers and developers. The group works closely together with little contact with the base organization. But the organization expects that eventually they shall present a product or products to be developed further for production and marketing that will ultimately result in increasing the organization's profitability. The project then moves into a new phase, where contact with the base organization will be intense.

These examples illustrate that projects very often have a need for contact between the project and people working in the base organization. Whether projects will be successful or not depends on a common understanding of the significance of the project and a common perception of how it should proceed. Therefore, a good project culture is important for the success of both PSO projects and projects that initially do not proceed like typical PSO projects.

A good project culture requires a joint effort from line management, steering committees, project management, elected employee representatives, and anyone who performs work, large or small, in projects. This interaction is absolutely fundamental. We will look first at top management.

TOP MANAGEMENT

Organizations have many projects running concurrently today, and we can easily foresee this increasing in the future. Top management has responsibility for the whole volume of projects.

We have known for a long time that it is important to run each project, whether it is an IT project, an engineering development project or something else, in an excellent way. This book will help you to manage your projects even better. Everyone does not succeed equally well – we constantly read about failed projects. But many succeed; projects are finished at the right time and within budget, and create the desired effect in the base organization, among customers and clients.

But being successful on individual projects is no longer good enough for the organization. The organization must succeed with all its projects. We mean that the effect of the total volume of projects must be something more than the sum of the single projects. To succeed, the organization must have a carefully prepared strategy, choose the right projects, be conscious of and exploit the connection between them, allocate resources, and then carry through each project according to plan.

Organizations that can manage their entire portfolio of projects in a better way than their competitors will have an advantage. This is a primary responsibility of top management. As a minimum, top management must select the projects to be performed. Top management must be aware that through its choice of projects, it is making strategic decisions as to the direction of the organization.

As a start towards portfolio management, the organization must establish a common record of all its projects and update it on a regular basis. They should ensure that projects are managed in a relatively uniform way. For example, they may make a policy to run projects in accordance with the philosophy, principles, processes and tools described in this book (GDPM). When all the projects are following the same methodological approach one can make a meaningful list of them, in the sense that we can see how much they have progressed and discuss allocation of resources between them.

The subject of project management is changing character. The focus is no longer on just individual projects. Project management has matured to the point of being concerned with how the organization should manage project management, which includes project portfolio management and selecting the right projects to reach its organizational objectives and implement its strategy.

Good management of individual projects will continue to be very important, and many people have made it their career path of choice. The management of an enterprise, whether it is a private organization or a public institution, must have greater knowledge, skills, and attitudes about the projects. The 'new' project subject puts additional demands on top management and on those who advise them.

LINE MANAGEMENT

Line management will be involved in project work either because they have personnel responsibility for people who work on projects, or because they will participate in or contribute to the professional decision-making processes in the project.

Our ideal is the case where top management have prioritized and approved a project. Line managers make project support a part of their normal duty to the organization, even if they did not participate in sponsoring the project. Top management and line management together must disseminate information to the staff in the base organization on the priorities behind the decisions to back projects in the portfolio. They must show why the projects are important to the base organization.

The line manager's task is to carry through agreed commitments regarding the project. They mainly consist of making professional decisions at the right time and making agreed-upon personnel resources available for the duration of the project. The line managers must be loyal to whatever has been agreed upon and documented on the principle and milestone responsibility charts. They must support the project in word and by deed.

When the project manager and line management have worked out a responsibility chart and agreed that a specific decision-making process should take place during the last half of April, this really means that the decision should be made before 1 May. It should have been thoroughly discussed and each individual professional member affected should have had an opportunity to make his views known and should accept the decision taken. Line management must understand that delays create huge problems. The agreement also means that the decision is binding, except for certain unforeseen circumstances.

In PSO projects, most project members are subordinate to a line manager. This means that the project manager does not have the full authority to determine when they should work on the project. If access to personnel resources must not be a major problem for the project manager, the line managers must see to it that people are available for the project as agreed. The line manager must ensure that people take over the project members' tasks in the base organization while they are working on the project. Release must be more than just a casual agreement; there must be a cover plan.

Participation in the project and project results are also important for the base organization. Therefore, line managers must motivate their staff to work earnestly on projects. People from the base organization should also be assessed on their contributions to projects as part of their routine performance evaluations.

It is easy for line management to assert that they do not have resources to spare for project work. This is especially the case in organizations with a poorly developed project culture and with little understanding of the importance of change and development.

The problem is aggravated if there are only a few staff members who are regarded as possible project members. They will keep turning up like 'a bad penny' in connection with projects. An organization that wants a good project culture and understands the importance of using the project approach should broaden its project expertise. By doing this, it will be able to draw from more people when it recruits for project work.

If an organization does not seem to have the resources for prioritized projects, the following questions may help find a solution:

- In large one-off tasks undertaken previously (they may not have been called projects), how were resources found?
- In current one-off tasks in progress at present, is the priority as high as the priority of projects the organization now wants to undertake?
- Of all the non-recurring work, actual and potential, what are the priority tasks for the organization?
- How are resources being used in the organization? Are they being wasted, for example, in non-productive meetings?

The organization should realize the significance of development work and systematically make decisions to free resources for this. As a rule, there is always room for some development work. Staff members are often willing, and in many cases eager, to participate in development projects. They see projects as an opportunity for a change of pace and a challenge in comparison with their daily routine work. They will make great efforts to be included in projects even if they are fully occupied with their daily work. They might work discretionary overtime to be able to participate in those project tasks. This obviously is not the most satisfactory solution. A good project culture means that resources are made available as a matter of priority and not just as a matter of goodwill.

PROJECT OWNER

The project owner is the person from the base organization who has the main responsibility for the project. The project owner will often be a representative from top management or line management, depending on the project's significance and scope.

The project is executed for the project owner. He is responsible for approving the project's mandate, milestone plan and milestone responsibility chart. He must also approve the economic plan for the project. He receives milestone reports, which form the basis for his control over the progress of the project.

In some organizations it is normal to appoint a steering committee for a project. Such a group takes on the responsibilities as described above. It is our opinion that lines of responsibility would be clearer in a project if there were only a project owner and no steering committee. However, a project owner may be the chairman of the steering committee. We discuss the role of steering committees below and shall discuss the necessity of having them.

STEERING COMMITTEE

Role and responsibility of the steering committee

The steering committee plays a central role in a project. Its main responsibilities are to initiate and propose the project, approve the principle responsibility chart, approve the milestone plan, and approve the milestone responsibility chart. It should determine the use of resources and ensure that the principle and milestone responsibility charts are observed.

If those in positions of responsibility are clearly delineated on the responsibility chart, and the role of the base organization is clearly described, is a steering committee still necessary? In many cases it is. But in some cases this group is not necessary.

A significant issue for the project approach is dependency on resources from the base organization. Even if it is absolutely clear which resources must be provided, in practice it is not so easy to do. In this situation, a steering committee can be beneficial. It could be comprised of a group of line managers to ensure that the relationship between the base organization and the project functions as it should. These line manager colleagues can ensure that everyone sticks to agreements made. They can also find solutions for problems regarding access to resources. It may be easier for a group of line managers to tackle these problems than for a project manager to take them up with each line manager in turn.

This example also shows that the line managers who are involved in the project should be included in the steering committee. It is not usual for elected employee representatives to be on the steering committee.

If the project involves the staff of only one line manager, then it is natural that this line manager be the 'steering committee'. The responsibility chart would show that this manager is assigned all the operational tasks belonging to a steering committee.

Usually a project involves several areas of responsibility and project personnel are then usually responsible to several line managers. If the managers involved meet frequently as a manager group, they could also function as a steering committee for the project. Part of the management group's meeting should then be used as a steering committee meeting. We see no reason to establish a new forum unless absolutely necessary. It simplifies administration, and we can assume that people who are used to working together will function better as a group.

Some organizations decide that their management board should function as a steering committee for all projects involving more than one sector. The board then makes time for steering committee tasks each time they assemble.

Some companies have so much experience using the project approach that they have little need to establish a steering committee. Relevant tasks are simply divided among those involved according to their areas of responsibility and described on the responsibility charts.

We present two situations where a steering committee is essential. They are when: 1) the project approach is unknown in the base organization; 2) the project crosses organizational limits or involves several companies.

If the organization does not have any experience with project work, it is particularly important to give prestige and support to the project and the project manager. This can be achieved to a greater extent by establishing a steering committee than distributing its tasks to a series of individuals. Since the steering committee consists of some or all line managers, it will be perceived as a forum with authority, and its pronouncements will have credibility.

If line management is not used to working with projects, it may be difficult in many cases to ensure that it will accept its responsibilities for the projects. When matters are discussed in a steering committee with several line managers, it is easier to get individual line managers to realize their responsibilities. Line managers are more aware of their responsibilities when they see that others also take on similar responsibilities. The same matters can, of course, be expressed on the responsibility charts, but the dialogue between the participants in a steering committee ensures that the commitments are felt more deeply.

In an organization lacking project experience, training and motivation are important. It is particularly important that knowledge and expertise come in at the top level. In such a situation, a steering committee can be used deliberately to provide training in project work. When central people in the base organization belong to a steering committee, it can be used to give project members skills and shared attitudes.

If the project is a joint venture for several organizations, a steering committee is essential. One example could be that several firms within the same line of business join forces to purchase hardware and software to solve a common data-processing task. In such a case, one executive from a single organization does not preside over the decision, but rather executives from all the companies collaborate on the project. Some decisions must be made jointly, and that requires a steering committee.

Let us look a little more closely at the steering committee's tasks. It will have tasks relating to the base organization. First and foremost it should ensure that it lives up to its commitments. It should ensure that resources are released and the decisions made as agreed. The steering committee must:

- ensure that the right people are chosen for the project tasks;
- ensure that the project is prioritized on the basis of the organization's needs, if circumstances arise in the base organization that create resource problems and individual line managers want to curtail the project;
- contribute to finding solutions if access to resources falters;
- monitor the decision-making processes in the base organization to ensure they function as agreed. It must be on guard against decisions made too slowly or too quickly and it must counteract tendencies among line managers to serve only their own interests.

The steering committee should carry out quality control for plans, progress, and results produced by the project manager and team. The steering committee must:

- contribute to motivation and team spirit in the project;
- acknowledge when milestones and project goals are reached – rewards are often in short supply;
- ensure that project management functions at a high level of quality.

From what has been said so far, it is clear that an appointment to a steering committee is not an 'honorary title' but an important job. The steering committee has management responsibility, a high-level responsibility for the project's success.

The steering committee should not make professional or technical decisions, but ensure that there are high-quality plans and decision-making processes. It should assist the project manager by seeing to it that the decision-makers and resource providers fulfil their obligations at the times agreed. This imposes considerable demands and expectations on the steering committee. The leader of the group has a special responsibility to make certain that it lives up to its responsibilities. Good work on the part of the steering committee can be measured by a better project culture in the organization.

Dangers of having steering committee

There is a fundamental difference between a steering committee and a decision-making group. In general we are against decision-making groups in project work. They imply that the people who have professional responsibility in the base organization are deprived of that responsibility, that it is transferred instead to a group, which is usually less competent than those who deal with such matters on a daily basis. The establishment of a decision-making group conflicts with one of the central principles for project work, namely that as far as possible professional decisions follow the normal decision-making process. A decision-making group has negative consequences both for the quality of decisions and for motivation in the base organization to accept those decisions.

There is an acknowledged danger that a steering committee can easily develop into a decision-making group. This is the greatest problem with steering committees.

In many cases the people who are to make professional decisions belong to the steering committee. But it is important for steering committee members to state that they make professional decisions as a line manager and not as a member of the steering committee. And if there is a need for decisions to be made jointly by several line managers, where they all perhaps belong to the steering committee, then this decision should not be made within the framework of the steering committee's tasks. It is a group of line managers exercising their authority.

Even though we strongly emphasize that the steering committees should not make professional decisions that belong in the base organization, it does happen all too often, nevertheless. It has serious consequences for the base organization's attitude towards the project. We get what we call 'denial of responsibility in the base organization'. This means that it does not feel any commitment to the decisions made. Difficult decisions must often be made in a project. If a line manager feels that he can avoid making some decisions because the steering committee encroaches on his territory, he may just let it happen and wait and see whether the steering committee's decision was right or not.

It is easy for a line manager to push decisions that are his responsibility over to the steering committee if the steering committee does not adhere to the principle of keeping out of the base organization's area of responsibility. You will then hear the

chorus from the base organization saying: 'But we've got a steering committee that makes all the decisions.'

If the steering committee is also a decision-making group,
there will be a slow decision-making process. The problem is
partly due to a well-known phenomenon; it is difficult to get a
lot of busy people together for a meeting, at least at short notice.
At the same time, often when these meetings are convened,
many decisions will be deferred till the meeting. There is thus a
tendency for business to be deferred until the next meeting.
The result is that a considerable period of time passes before
decisions are made.

Nevertheless, there are situations where it is proper for the
steering committee also to function as a decision-making group.
The most important case is when the project is a joint project for
several independent organizations. Certain professional decisions have a great impact on the project costs, and since they will
be distributed among several organizations, it is a matter for the
steering committee to make a decision on professional questions
that have a significant influence on costs. In less critical matters,
one may establish decision-making groups with representatives
from all the participating organizations, so that those who have
daily responsibility for a particular area in their own group agree
jointly on the best solutions.

Operation of the steering committee

When a steering committee is established, one must not assume
that it will know how to organize its work. Neither is it obvious
that the participants have the necessary skills to perform steering committee functions. Often, several participants in the steering committee have not done such work before. Project
management differs from management of the base organization.
Experiences from normal line management cannot automati-
cally be transferred to work in a steering committee.

Lack of experience in steering committee work often leads to
unstructured discussions, continual conflicts of interest, and
advocacy of individual obsessions. The steering committee often
has a representative composition; it consists of those line
managers who have interests in the project. They are people

who represent the various parties involved in the project. They sometimes see taking care of the interests of their unit in the base organization as being their main task. As an introduction to the project a positive atmosphere can be created by discussing and clarifying different interests and matters of conflict. The fact that there are differing views on how high a priority a project is or the direction it should take must not be regarded as negative.

The mandate with its purpose and goals, the milestone plan and the milestone responsibility chart are tools that can be used to clarify special interests and to define precisely the participation of the different parties in the project. A high level of involvement in these discussions is very good. However, there is a problem if the steering committee is continually used for airing conflicts or promoting factional interests. Often, individual parties continue to bring up the same 'old' arguments that they brought up during the planning stage. In this case, the steering committee will likely make little to no progress. Instead of monitoring the progress of the project, members of the committee will become bogged down in discussing high-level questions that should have been decided upon earlier and they will continue to pursue their own interests instead of considering the project.

It is important to determine whether the steering committee members have the necessary skills to function well. If they are lacking, special training measures can be introduced.

As mentioned previously, project management and line management are different. It may be necessary for new steering committee participants, including those with extensive administrative experience, to receive special training in the special tasks belonging to a steering committee. They should not perceive this as a criticism; however, they may resist this training because they may perceive this as damaging their prestige. Therefore, it may be necessary to integrate the training into some form of start-up meeting for the project, thereby camouflaging it with a number of other simultaneous project activities.

The efficiency of the steering committee also depends on the project manager. The way in which a project manager works with a steering committee determines the results of its work. It is very important that the project manager knows what constitutes appropriate matters for the steering committee. He must be very certain about what matters the steering committee should deal with and what it should not. The project manager greatly influences the steering committee's effectiveness by his ability to lay a good foundation for the group's decision-making. He must make sure that the steering committee receives documents in enough time before a meeting, and that each item on the agenda is thoroughly organized. The project manager must actively contribute towards developing an efficient working style of the steering committee. It is expedient to have:

- set days for meetings planned at least six months ahead;
- certain permanent items on the agenda;
- minutes with a predetermined structure.

It may seem a small practical detail to establish steering committee meeting days six months ahead of time, but in fact it is not a trivial matter. Often, steering committee members are people heavily burdened with meetings. It is important to establish dates for steering committee meetings while the participants still have openings in their schedules. Furthermore, it should be emphasized to members that missing a steering committee meeting has implications for project progress and makes the steering committee jointly responsible for any project delay. If the project is to be taken seriously, 'death and funerals' are just about the only valid grounds for absence from meetings.

Permanent agenda items for all meetings contribute to firmly establishing the main tasks of the steering committee. This helps everyone understand that these are the central issues. The most important item on the agenda will be the progress of the project compared with the milestone plan. If the project is lagging behind schedule, the steering committee must discuss what actions should be taken to correct the situation. The project manager must keep the milestone plan and the milestone responsibility chart alive at every steering committee meeting by referring to them and relating them to all discussions.

In addition to permanent items, the agenda may, of course, also contain problems brought forward by the project since the last steering committee meeting. The group should be informed of the problems and take an appropriate action.

It is important that minutes be sent out relatively quickly after each meeting stating clearly the actions decided upon and who has been assigned the responsibility for executing them. This is vital for steering committee meetings. Late minutes can easily create the impression that 'there is a lot of time'. If the steering committee is not disciplined, it cannot expect others to be.

The minutes must state the steering committee's decisions (approved plans, changes to plans, actions, etc). The minutes are documents that project members will use in their work. It is of lesser importance to report the debate leading up to the decisions. This will often contribute to much longer minutes and will also focus on disagreements within the steering committee, something that is not necessary for the project team to know. In certain cases, however, it is necessary to report the background on which the decisions were taken, so those reading the minutes from the meeting understand and accept the decisions. We recommend that a set form be developed for the minutes to make them easy to read and understand by the project members.

Tasks of the steering committee

In the previous sections we discussed the steering committee's tasks. We will conclude by relating the tasks to the tools that we suggest in this book. The tasks of the steering committee are shown in Figure 10.2.

The principle responsibility chart depicts guidelines for how project work is to be conducted in the organization. These guidelines may be applied to all the projects in the organization, and should be authorized by the organization's top management.

The project decisions that should be taken by the steering committee may be specified on the principle responsibility chart. Decisions concerning the project's goals, limitations and finances are especially important to the steering committee.

It is the steering committee's task to approve the milestone plan and to ensure that the project follows it. The milestone plan is the most important planning document in the project and it makes sense for the steering committee to be responsible for it as the project's top authority. In following up on progress against the milestone plan, the steering committee carries out its central

The steering committee shall:
- Approve the mandate (if it isn't already decided on by the project owner before the steering committee is established).
- Approve the principle responsibility chart (there may be one that applies generally to all projects in the organization, in which case the steering committee does not need to discuss it).
- Approve the milestone plan.
- Approve the milestone responsibility chart.
- Be responsible for ensuring that the project follows the principle responsibility chart, milestone responsibility chart and the milestone plan.

Figure 10.2 The formal tasks of the steering committee

progress control function. If the plan cannot be followed, the steering committee must decide whether changes should be made in the milestone plan, or whether corrective measures should be introduced. The project manager is responsible for preparing the basis for the steering committee's decisions. This applies both to the milestone plan and the milestone reports upon which control is based.

The steering committee should be responsible for the global organization of the project. The milestone responsibility chart expresses the organization. It therefore makes sense for the steering committee to approve it. It must also take action on any variances against what was agreed upon. It is the steering committee's responsibility to ensure that the project follows the milestone responsibility chart. However, it is not the steering committee's task to set up the milestone responsibility chart. The project manager does this in cooperation with the people and parties who will carry out the work, but again, final approval rests with the steering committee.

PROJECT MANAGER

The project manager manages the project on a day-to-day basis. He must plan the work, organize it and ensure that corrective measures are taken so that the project finishes within time and budget. The project manager must also re-evaluate the plan if access to resources is not as expected.

The project manager must organize work internally within the project and in relation to the base organization. He must arrange for effective interfaces between the project and the base organization.

The project manager must anticipate events. He cannot expect that project members will just appear when the project needs them. He must plan, negotiate with line managers, motivate, inspire, establish agreements on cooperation in the project, and see to it that the resources appear at the right time.

Project management is different from line management, and it demands other skills. This book is an introduction to methods and tools that are used in project work, and are usually unfamiliar to line managers. It is a characteristic skill for project managers to manage people who do not work together on a daily basis, and therefore do not know each other in the same way as colleagues in the base organization. The project manager must create a sense of community among people who are initially strangers to each other.

Project management should be regarded as a distinct profession requiring specialized knowledge and skills. Most people accept the fact that they cannot become a line manager until they have gone through a basic 'apprenticeship' where they acquire the relevant knowledge, experience and interpersonal insights. But it is rather depressing to see organizations set high standards for its line management and then not expect high standards for its project managers, including those managing very important projects.

In general, too little effort goes into developing good project managers. Project management is often more difficult than line management (eg unknown tasks and unfamiliar people). One would expect higher requirements for project managers than for line managers regarding training and experience.

The project manager should be educated in the field of project management. It is now possible to acquire basic professional skills through courses and training programmes. Experience as a 'rank and file' project member is also necessary.

An organization should spend time and money training its project managers. One cannot become a line manager without a solid background – but some believe that anybody can be a project manager.

Qualities of the project manager

One sometimes sees specifications for the personal qualities required of a project manager. He should, for example, have distinct leadership qualities (charisma), be 'loved' by his team, have the ability to communicate with superiors and subordinates and be able to represent the project externally in a very favourable manner. Such lists often give a picture of a person who is superhuman, and are usually of little practical use. There is no sense in dreaming away and demanding supernatural qualities of a project manager. When an organization must choose a project manager for a project, it is necessary to choose from among those who are available.

The project manager's personal character is important, but for most practical purposes there is little value in comparing a person with a list of super qualities. Instead it is important to have an idea of the essential requirements for a project manager's success. And since it is often extremely difficult to know whether a person will succeed as a project manager, it is also useful to know what type of person should be avoided absolutely.

A project manager must be capable of formulating a realistic description of the present situation in the project. Concurrently, he must be able to manage variances between current and desired future states. He should also have the ability to envision what types of measures will be effective.

The project manager must observe progress in the project very closely. He must be able to assess the situation realistically. A dreamer (who only sees through 'rose-coloured glasses') or an optimist (who believes that everything will sort itself out as it goes along) is of no use.

Realism in the evaluation of the present situation must apply to both factual matters and people. The control criteria that we described earlier are of course very useful tools for developing an accurate description of the present situation. They are first and foremost factual. That is, they report developments in relation to the project's plans and goals. They are to a lesser degree oriented to the welfare of the team. However, the project manager must be concerned with both factual and people matters. He must be able to sense the mood of the project and form a realistic picture of the team members' situation. He must support them and assist them in the realization of their goals. He must push reserved people forward and control dominant ones.

In general, a project manager must have a flexible nature, so that he will be able to change course along the way. He must be action oriented and willing to try new measures if there is a deviation between the plan and reality. Through a constant evaluation of what works and what does not work, what is helpful and what is not (including his own contributions), a project manager must continually improve his competency. In other words, he must be a good learner.

We hope that we have not just described a new superhuman. We do not believe so. We have indicated the importance for project managers to:

- give realistic assessments of project situations, concerning both factual and people matters;
- propose and implement actions to correct situations, concerning both factual and people matters;
- learn what types of measures are effective, concerning both factual and people matters.

An important aspect in choosing project managers is to avoid people who are not really suited for the job. We will describe three types who are dangerous for any project. They are the technocrat, the bureaucrat and the salesman. The descriptions below will perhaps seem to be caricatures, but they contain important truths.

Firstly, a little about the technocrat. The most able programmer seldom makes a good project manager for an IT project. He is so preoccupied with programming skills that he has neither the time, desire nor ability to practise project management. Project management does not mean doing the job yourself, but seeing to it that others do. Super-technocrats are dangerous as project managers because they believe – with some reason – that they can do everything best themselves. They do not actually want others to interfere in the work. They also often lack the personal qualities that enable them to get people to pull together as a group. The technocrat's strength lies at the technical level – not at the human level. Able technocrats are very important in projects, but not as project managers.

The bureaucrat is the person who regards project administration as being the essence of the project. He loves forms and reports. He is obviously a torment to those around him, especially those who do not follow procedures to the letter. Worse, however, is that he does not make any worthwhile use of all this paperwork. It does not form the basis for any action; it just accumulates in filing cabinets. When project members feel that reports are more important than the product they are producing, motivation falls drastically.

The salesman is the project manager who is all talk. Externally the project is presented as a real success – internally little is happening. It is obviously important to maintain the project's public profile and to create enthusiasm for and interest in it. Yet all the talk is wasted if the project manager does not manage to follow it up with concrete plans and action. Unfortunately, there are far too many examples of projects that remain 'castles in the air'.

Tasks of the project manager

The project manager's main tasks are summarized in Figure 10.3.

The tasks are listed under the headings of planning, organization and control. There is a distinction between tasks at the global level and tasks at the detail level. Tasks at the global level involve the project manager's work with the steering committee or whoever is fulfilling the corresponding function; tasks at detail level include his work with the project team.

The central project planning task is to draw up the milestone plan. This is the project manager's responsibility. Final approval lies with the steering committee.

At the detail level, the project manager's main task is to manage the development of the activity plans, those plans covering the activities to obtain the different milestones. In addition, he must discuss how the individual activities should be done with those who will actually carry them out.

Planning tasks:

Foundation:	Manage development of mission breakdown structure, stakeholder analysis and mandate
Global level:	Manage development of milestone plan and uncertainty analysis
Detail level:	Manage development of activity plans (activity responsible chart)

Organizational tasks:

Global level:	Manage development of milestone responsibility chart
Detail level:	Manage daily operations

Control tasks:

Global level:	Monitor that the principle responsibility chart and milestone responsibility chart are being followed
	Prepare the milestone reports
Detail level:	Follow up on the activity reports

Figure 10.3 The main tasks of the project manager

Global organization of the project is a significant task for the project manager. He has to develop a proposal for a milestone responsibility chart and present it to the steering committee for approval. The project manager leads the daily operations of the project. It is his task to ensure that work goes on day to day. He is also responsible for prioritizing and assigning tasks that are not included in the plans. He must motivate and support his team.

A project manager should have professional qualifications in the field covered by the project, although there may be exceptions in very large projects. We feel that the project manager should be an 'active coach'; he should be able to direct and perform special work related to his professional area. This does not mean that he should be able to do more than everyone else, but he should be sufficiently qualified to be able to lead professional discussions in the project. We believe that a project manager who is unfamiliar with the professional issues in the project will lack the respect of his team.

The project manager must be able to guarantee the quality of the results produced by the project. In order to be able to do this he should preferably have a professional background that will enable him to judge the quality of the results. (Note that there is a great difference between performing a job and judging its quality; there is a difference between ski-jumping and awarding marks for the style of the jump.) In certain areas, it may be appropriate for others to carry out quality control. Nevertheless, it is essential that the project manager has a background that enables him to see the difference between good and poor quality.

The project manager must ensure that the milestone responsibility chart is followed in the project work. He must report the variances that he cannot handle by himself to the steering committee.

The project manager must present milestone reports to the steering committee. There may be several reasons for variances between a milestone plan and the actual project situation. The project manager has the authority to resolve certain matters and others must be submitted to the steering committee or appropriate decision authorities for resolution.

If a project manager considers that the project cannot achieve its purpose or goals, he has the duty to tell the steering committee that the project should be terminated. If they act on his recommendation, they must not make him the 'scapegoat' when he has done his duty and taken the initiative to stop in time.

The project manager also has a duty to inform the steering committee regarding poor resources supplied by the base organization and the impacts to the project's progress.

Controlling the activities is the project manager's responsibility. Project members provide the project manager with the basis for his activity reports. He must take the initiative himself to initiate action if reports indicate deviation from the plan.

We have concentrated on the hard aspects of the project manager's tasks. In addition, we strongly emphasize the project manager's responsibility for the 'climate' in the project. This means being concerned both with the situations of individual team members and the interaction between them.

The project manager is responsible for developing the project team. This is, perhaps, the most important job of all. He must stimulate, motivate, and secure good cooperation from day to day so that everyone helps each other in their efforts to achieve common goals. He must get everyone involved in the project – steering committee, the top executives, line managers, project members, elected trade union representatives – to work together for the project. This responsibility is not as clearly structured as the tasks we examined earlier in this section – but it is just as important.

Where there is a spirit of community in a project, where everyone is prepared to help each other in finding solutions for delays
instead of allocating blame, an important cooperative goal has
been reached. This demands great things of project management. It demands a motivating and supportive management
style, not an authoritarian one.

Permanent project managers?

This is an issue that only troubles larger organizations constantly
engaged with some sort of development work. They face the
question of whether they should have permanent project
managers. The alternative is to let the project manager return to
his usual job in the base organization, at least for a time.

Permanent project managers have both advantages and
drawbacks. The advantages are very clear. The project
managers expand their knowledge of, and gain broad experience in, project management. As permanent project managers
they have greater opportunities to use what they have learnt in
a succession of projects. With a permanent group of project
managers it is also possible to put into effect measures aimed at
professionalizing project management. By having the same
project managers for several projects, all the projects in the
organization will benefit from a more uniform approach. It will
become easier to exchange experience between projects and to
use the experience from one project to achieve still better results
in the next.

A project manager who gains experience from several types of
project and from different areas within an organization will also
gradually acquire a deeper understanding of the base organization's culture. He will see how the organization functions and
how management is exercised at different levels. The project
manager thus has a good background for formulating proposals
for solving problems within the base organization; he understands what can be done, and what will work.

One drawback of permanent project managers is that they
become an institution in the organization. In this position they
acquire power or influence and in many situations it becomes
natural to ask for their opinions. If they become too highly insti-

tutionalized, antagonism can easily develop between them and the rest of the base organization. This is a poor basis for cooperation when a new project gets under way.

Previously we have stressed the importance of a project manager having professional expertise within the field of the project. When permanent project managers manage all projects within the organization, you may have project managers who have little or no professional connection with the area of the project. This is a weakness that must be balanced against the strength of having a trained project manager.

A decision must be made on where to place permanent project managers in the base organization. Here are two alternatives: 1) under different line managers, but still functioning as a group; 2) in a joint staff unit that reports to the managing director. The latter solution makes it is easier to professionalize project management.

ELECTED REPRESENTATIVES

In some countries, laws give elected employee representatives the right to joint consultation in development projects that alter the content and organization of the workplace.

Further, there can be a range of different forums and official bodies that ought to have a role in certain projects. We mention:

- trade unions (sometimes several);
- a work environment committee;
- a health and safety committee.

The groups vary from organization to organization. Their roles also differ greatly: some are established by formal agreement; others are more dependent on practices in the individual organization. Practice varies widely from country to country also. In some places, employee representatives assume responsibilities that would be culturally unacceptable elsewhere.

Therefore, it must be up to each organization and each project to determine roles and responsibilities. Unless these are made clear, the employees' representatives may not acquire a role anywhere and may be omitted from the project.

If the elected representatives are to fulfil their responsibilities as such, they must choose carefully their areas of activity. In unstructured projects, there is a tendency for the elected representatives to try to be a part of everything. They may fear that something will happen behind their backs, or they may not know what they need to concentrate on.

There are four matters that should be of particular interest for elected representatives:

- priorities for proposed projects and decisions on which projects should be started;
- the principle responsibility chart;
- the milestone plan, especially in projects that have an impact on future employment;
- the milestone responsibility chart.

The first two apply to project work in general, while the last two are linked to individual projects.

An organization's projects are of decisive significance for its future. It is natural that the employees' representatives have views on which projects the organization ought to prioritize.

The principle responsibility chart shows the main division of tasks in projects. The various employee interest groups must be assigned the correct roles.

The milestone plan with its result paths shows what the project should achieve. The employees' representatives must have an opportunity to put forward their views on the plan. They ought to pay particular attention to whether or not the plan takes into consideration anything affecting future employment.

The detailed responsibilities of elected representatives as set out in the milestone responsibility chart will vary greatly according to national and organizational practice as well as the specifics of the project. They may be consulted on a wide range of issues concerning employment and the working environment and these will be reflected in 'C's in the chart. This does not confer powers of decision or veto, of course, and if the representatives do not agree with what is decided, they may take it up with top management outside the context of the project organization.

Some elected representatives misunderstand their function and believe that they should be included as much as possible –

even at meetings where the detailed technical matters are discussed. This impairs their ability to do the real job they have in the project.

The danger of an elected representative being preoccupied with detail is greatest when they have experience and expertise in the particular area within which the project is working. Elected representatives are drawn from the base organization and are often very capable within their fields. Many are therefore tempted to express opinions on how detail activities ought to be executed. This is a clear misuse of the role of elected representative. It may be relevant to draw on their specific expertise, but that is in a completely different context. In that event, it should be stressed that the person concerned is acting as a professional consultant or as a future user. It is very important that an elected representative who is used in this way does not confuse this task with his role as elected representative.

A PROJECTIVITY PROGRAMME

Projectivity is an organization's ability to achieve results using the project approach. The word is designed to provide associations with the words effective, productivity and project. If the organization is to improve its projectivity, it must work consciously toward this goal. In this section we will look more closely at the elements of a projectivity programme; in other words, we will look at a development plan to improve projectivity in the base organization.

The following conditions must always exist for such a programme to be successful.

The base organization's top management must support the programme

Support means something more than management deciding that the programme should be started. They should also have understood what the programme implies by way of involvement for themselves and others. They must really want such a programme because they realize the importance of mastering the project approach.

A project manager must be designated for the programme

There must be one person who has experience both as a project manager and with GDPM as a method. He must have easy access to top management and command great respect from the other project managers in the organization.

The programme must be planned and organized like other projects

It must be divided up into phases and have a duration of at least a year. All projects that are at an appropriate stage of development must be included, ie those that have reached a stage where a milestone plan and a responsibility chart can be drawn up. The worst thing is to select simple, small projects as tests. They will not receive the necessary attention. In any case, the real problems will not be revealed. If the number of projects must be limited, at least do not exclude the most important, the largest and the most difficult ones.

Before launching a projectivity programme, a certain amount of groundwork must be done. Top management must have approved a foundation, which forms the basis for all project work in the organization. It must specify at least:

- the base organization's purpose for using the project approach;
- policies for project work, in other words the fundamental guidelines for directing each project;
- the chosen method for directing project work (we presuppose that GDPM will be chosen);
- the various procedures to be followed in project work;
- documentation requirements for project work.

The document that describes the foundation for project work should apply to the whole organization – line management, line members, project management and project members – and also to external collaborating parties. It is the common basis for project work and also expresses how project quality will be assured within the base organization. It states the level of ambition and provides the framework for the projectivity programme.

At an early stage in the work on improving projectivity, the base organization's project culture should be mapped. One must understand what hinders and what promotes projectivity in the existing project culture. Different projects in the organization must be examined. There are often great dissimilarities between the different categories of projects (product development, computer and organization development projects, and purely technical projects). There may also be great differences in maturity in relation to project work in different parts of the base organization. It may be relevant to: 1) ask all members of the base organization to fill out a questionnaire; 2) interview a representative selection from the various categories of people. The results will reveal the base organization's project culture. It provides a basis for proposing actions and provides a direction for further work in the projectivity programme.

An organization cannot implement such a programme with too many project managers. It may be necessary to limit the number, both to achieve a manageable development programme and to secure high-quality project managers. On the other hand, neither can an organization have too few trained project managers. They ought to have a professional connection with the area within which their projects are working – and that requires a number of project managers who actively use the project approach. Reorganization of project management, good organizational support and selection of the best project managers are normally important elements in a successful programme.

Project managers receive special treatment in a projectivity programme and will be the recipients of a structured development programme. The purpose is to bring the project managers up to a fully professional level in planning, organization, control, team development and base organization cooperation.

As a link in the development programme the project managers should work on arranging the next year's prioritization of the organization's many projects. The project manager forum can also serve as a review group for new milestone plans and responsibility charts.

It may be appropriate to give formal certification to project managers when they have reached a desired level of proficiency. An independent body should carry out certification. It should inspect the finished projects and their results. The project manager's input should be judged on the basis of the quality of:

- milestone plans and responsibility charts;
- activity planning;
- progress reporting to management;
- project control, at project level and activity level;
- team development in the project;
- relations with line managers;
- handling of the decision-making process.

When top management have initiated a projectivity programme, they must also take an interest in it and follow up its results. The project manager for the programme must make it easy for management to involve themselves in the work. There should be at least one meeting a month between the project manager and top management, where the progress of the programme and current projects included in it are dealt with.

The line managers in the base organization must also be enabled to play their part; they can raise the quality of project plans by expressing their views and ideas. They can contribute to securing quality in project work by taking decisions as agreed and ensuring that their people are released for project work to the agreed extent and at the time agreed. They should cooperate closely with the project managers, both as a means of helping in the various projects, but also as a means of helping to develop and strengthen the managers themselves as a part of the projectivity programme.

For those parts of the organization where initial studies showed a poorly developed project culture, it may be relevant to initiate a specific development programme within the framework of the projectivity programme. This may apply to departments or groups where there is a need to build up respect for deadlines and quality of work. They may also require assistance in such things as drawing up plans and taking action to release resources.

Project meetings in individual projects are important forums for team development. The programme's project manager should participate in these meetings as a process adviser and observer. The project participants must be encouraged to take up questions that concern team working and relationships and find solutions for such problems jointly. The group must be trained to be more disciplined and structured in their methods.

All people in the base organization should be offered a course in project methods. For line managers and their subordinates this may require one or two days.

The projectivity programme must be evaluated along the way by assessing quarterly individual project results and status. It is particularly important to determine whether:

- completion dates are being adhered to;
- resource utilization agrees with the original estimates;
- the level of ambition remains the same or whether it has been expanded or reduced.

Besides this, an assessment should be made of whether the project culture has improved. At the conclusion of the formal projectivity programme, it may be relevant to do a further review of project culture like the one carried out as an introduction to the programme.

11

Goal Directed Project Management – example and summary

In this chapter, we will look at an example of applying GDPM. Firstly, we will refer to forms that can help you in your work. IT support is also a great advantage in this type of work. We will go through a fictitious example where we will show the use of the forms and IT support. We will finish this chapter by appraising how GDPM satisfies the requirements for good project management and by showing how an organization improves its project performance.

FORMS

Complex project work requires methodological support. When the project has decided to use a specific project management method, all possible support for that method should be utilized. For instance, it is desirable to utilize carefully prepared forms for all documents. In GDPM forms are prepared for:

- mission breakdown structure;
- stakeholder analysis;
- project mandate;
- milestone plan, covering both plan and report;
- uncertainty matrix;

- responsibility chart, covering responsibilities and roles, time scheduling and report (the form is applicable to principle, milestone and activity responsibility charts).

The example below shows what these forms look like. To make the mission breakdown structure one can use software designed to make an organization chart (for example, MS Organization Chart).

IT SUPPORT

No projects should be implemented without IT support. Use of IT in project work has several advantages:

- facilitates the work of documenting the project;
- better quality of documentation through built-in quality controls;
- easier to make changes in the documentation and keep track of different versions;
- easier to report;
- the documentation of the project is filed in one place and is electronically accessible – particularly important in projects where the participants are geographically dispersed;
- easier to impart relevant information to different stakeholders.

Planning and organizing the project should be carried out as group work. It is necessary that all participants know what is taking place and take an active part in influencing this.

IT tools are becoming more helpful in facilitating creative sessions. This is especially true in virtual projects where participants are geographically dispersed. IT support can secure participation from people not present by giving them the opportunity to present their views electronically. The IT tool can facilitate exchanges of views over the Internet by giving people the chance to change or modify the different documents.

IT support is of great importance when the result of the group work needs to be documented. When changes are relatively easy to make, people are more receptive to different points of view. Project documentation that is electronically available is a great advantage and simplifies the exchange and distribution of information. It also makes it easier for the people responsible for activities to send in their reports.

IT support for a particular project management method helps to ensure that people will use the method correctly. IT support usually has built-in quality controls, such as controlling the consistency between documents. IT support for GDPM will, for example, ensure that there is integration between the milestone plan and the milestone responsibility chart.

If all the projects of the base organization use the same IT support one can achieve additional advantages:

- uniform method of approach for all the projects of the base organization;
- encourage exchange of experience and edifying of knowledge;
- supports managing the portfolio of all projects in the organization;
- supports managing project resources across the organization.

Common IT support contributes to the establishment of a good project culture in the base organization. There are many tools available for IT support. Choosing IT support that is particularly designed for the project management method one wishes to use is a big advantage.

'Goal Director' is an example of IT support designed especially for GDPM. The software is marketed by GDPM Systems Ltd (for the record, two of the authors of this book are among the owners). More information about this useful tool is given at the organization's homepage: http://www.gdpmsystems.com/. There you will be offered a light, inexpensive version of the software and the full Web-accessible, comprehensive, enterprise version which includes project portfolio management.

In the example below you will find printouts from 'Goal Director'.

EXAMPLE PROJECT 'NEW POSSIBILITIES IN NEW PREMISES'

We will illustrate the GDPM method with a somewhat more demanding project. We have chosen to construct an example rather than use a real case (even though the example is inspired by a real project). This gives us the opportunity to bring out most lessons and present as many points as possible in an easily comprehensible manner.

We will look at an organization that is a market leader within a sector of the electronic and computer field. It has approximately 200 employees. The organization sells its products both to private individuals and to organizations. It provides training and offers maintenance for the products. At the outset it is located at three sites in Oslo, Norway. This is causing poor customer service and inefficient operations.

At the beginning of December a project manager was appointed and assigned the project of moving to new premises. The project was to complete before the end of the following year, as the lease agreements for the present three locations expired then. Management also decided that the organization should use the relocation and integration of operations to raise the total quality of the organization's work. The project was given a free hand with regard to renting or buying the new premises, although the majority believed that ownership was more appropriate. The project should follow the principles for project work according to the company's common principle responsibility chart (see Figure 4.9).

Our relocation example will illustrate the importance of a good description of the desired achievements of the project. The organization will not achieve better quality by moving if everything else remains the same. Before moving, the emphasis must be on the discussion of the purpose of the move. The plans must show which results are desired and then how to achieve them. The project plans must emphasize cooperation, training, and development of new attitudes. The project will be successful if it leads to fewer complaints from customers, increased turnover, and better performance on deliveries.

Mission breakdown structure

When starting a new project, the purpose of the project is the first thing to be discussed. We use a mission breakdown structure to help us to decide upon the scope and direction of the project.

We will look at the mission breakdown structure for our relocation example (Figure 11.1). The main purpose for the project is indicated to be: 'A service building with efficiency and quality on all levels'. This is placed in the top box of the mission breakdown structure.

The purpose describes the desired future situation for the organization. The mission breakdown structure shows what the new premises should represent for the base organization. There are, of course, many conditions that need to be in place in order to create the desired situation. The mission breakdown structure elaborates on all the conditions necessary to achieve the main purpose.

A thorough discussion is necessary before one is ready to formulate the purpose. Our organization wants a strong position in the market and good profitability, but that purpose is at too high a level in relation to our project. The purpose has to be on such a level that the project can contribute something definitively and directly. So we choose to put direct focus on the new premises by calling it a service building and describe what it should look like in order to fulfil the main purpose.

The mission breakdown structure has the following sub-purposes:

- financial and legal conditions in perfect order;
- premises with all the necessary facilities;
- quality in deliveries, technical services and training;
- staff members who are service minded;
- suitable organization;
- good and efficient work processes.

This mission breakdown structure shows that in order to have a service building that facilitates efficiency and quality there needs to be certain basic conditions in place (financial and legal matters) and some supporting functions (efficient work processes). They are placed on the breakdown structure on both sides of what we may consider the core purposes in terms of PSO thinking: staff members (p), premises and quality (s) and organization (o).

The mission breakdown structure shows what the organization wishes to accomplish in the new premises. At this stage of

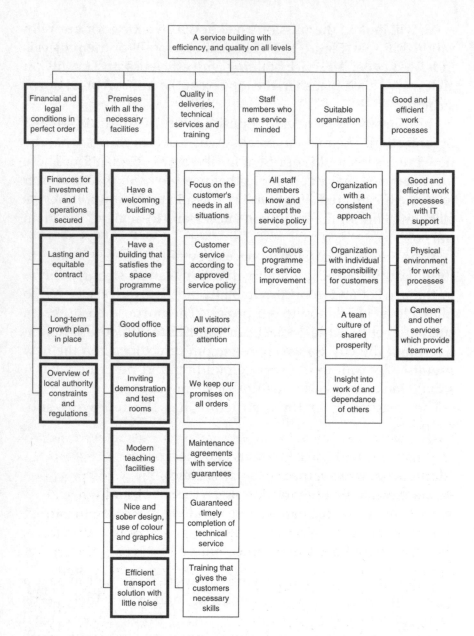

Figure 11.1 Mission breakdown structure with the project's responsibility clearly marked

the project, it is difficult to think through completely all the conditions that need to be in place to reach the main purpose. The mission breakdown structure is likely to have some short-comings. However, it is a good starting point for a discussion of what the project ought to be responsible for and what others ought to work with. Amendments can be added when new insights are gained.

The project does not need to be responsible for everything that the mission breakdown structure covers. This is not the point of the breakdown structure. It is a tool for dividing responsibilities between the project and the base organization.

It is not always easy to agree on the delegation of responsibilities. In practice, responsibilities must be clarified through discussions between the project (represented by the project owner and possibly the project manager) and the base organization (represented by the affected line managers).

In our example, the project is given the responsibility for:

* financial and legal conditions in perfect order;
* premises with all the necessary facilities;
* good and efficient work processes.

This seems to be a reasonable scope for the project. The project has the responsibility for acquiring new premises with the necessary facilities and sorting out all legal and financial matters. In addition, it has the responsibility of creating new work processes that will make the organization much more efficient when all its departments are located at one site. The base organization, however, has the responsibility of the quality of the sales force, the service and the training, and it must also develop the organizational structure and the attitudes of the organization staff.

When we have decided what responsibility the project shall have, we start the discussion of the goals for the project. But before we make our final decision on the goals, we should do a stakeholder analysis to get a perspective on who is interested in the project and what they expect from it.

Stakeholder analysis

A project has many stakeholders. The list in Figure 4.7 can help to identify the current project's stakeholders.

Stakeholder groupings can be made by identifying those stakeholders with the same interests. In many cases the organization employees are stakeholders, but in this case it appears to be necessary to differentiate between types of functions employees perform (sale, service, training) and their current geographic workplaces. The different categories of employees do not necessarily have the same views. For example, opinions on where the organization should move might depend on where the employees currently live and work.

We will not present a complete stakeholder analysis, but have included some stakeholders to illustrate what it will look like (Figure 11.2).

STAKEHOLDER ANALYSIS							
Name of project New possibilities in new premises			**Made by (date, name)** 15/11 Project manager Eve			**Approved by (date, name)** 16/12 Project owner	
Stake-holder	**Area of interest**	**Contri-butions**	**Expecta-tions**	**Power**	**Strategy**	**Respon-sible**	
Managing director	Finance, outcome of project	Decision on new premises	Increased sales and better market position	Can stop project	Must be involved	Project manager	
Sales staff	Location of new premises, organization of work	Increased motivation and service	Better workplace	Can work against project	Must be involved	Project manager	

Figure 11.2 Stakeholder analysis

Mandate

A mandate is prepared (Figure 11.3). The project name reflects what the project is about: 'New possibilities in new premises'. The mandate is based on the mission breakdown structure. The purpose is directly transferred from it. The three main goals in

Owner
Managing director

Background
Located at three different sites. Location creates problems. Should move to one site. Possible to create a more efficiency company. Could be more quality conscientious. Should use the relocation to improve work processes and service. Be more visible in the marketplace, also, by establishing a physical 'service building'.

Purpose
A service building with efficiency and quality on all levels

Scope
See the attached mission breakdown structure

Areas of work not included
See the attached mission breakdown structure

Goal
1. Premises with the necessary rooms and functionalities, which fulfil the service demands and make possible new and efficient work processes, are in use
2. New and efficient work processes with IT support are implemented
3. All necessary financial and legal agreements are settled

Constraints and guidelines
Must be settled in the new premises by the end of next year

Success criteria
A profitability analysis should be worked out, which shows good profitability of making the relocation

Figure 11.3 The mandate for the project 'New possibilities in new premises'

the project reflect that the project has the responsibility for three of the sub-purposes in the mission breakdown structure. The goals are not further described here. We are aware that the project will be divided into different phases and that it is easier to look at a detailed account of the goals for each phase.

Division into phases or sub-projects

This project has two clear phases: 1) work leading to the signing of the lease or purchase contract; 2) work from the time the premises have been selected until relocation is completed.

The first phase is mainly a feasibility study; the second phase is implementation. It is not particularly practical to plan the move before knowing the premises for the relocation. Therefore the project and the planning of it should be divided into at least these two phases.

We could further break down phases. The contract phase could be divided into two sub-phases: one phase developing the requirement specifications and another leading to contract signing. The first part is a pure feasibility study, while the second involves finding actual locations and selecting one of them. The implementation phase can be divided into two sub-phases, one that includes the physical fitting out, renovation and relocation, and one that includes purchasing and installing. For the simplicity of this example, we have not done this further subdividing.

Milestone plan for acquiring new premises

We will make the first phase that includes work leading to the signing of a contract a separate sub-project and plan it as such. This phase involves the acquisition of new premises. It is somewhat unimaginative to call the sub-project just that. Instead we will use the following wording: 'New premises for efficiency and prosperity'. The name describes to everyone what the purpose of the sub-project is. One is going to find a new location, but at the same time the new premises are to contribute to improved efficiency and prosperity.

In most cases, the mission breakdown structure makes it possible to draw up a considerably better milestone plan. It gives direction for good choices of result paths. The mission breakdown structure also assures us that all substantial dimensions of the project will be attended to.

The goals for the sub-project are not identical with the goals for the project. The sub-project will only bring the project a bit of the way towards completion. The sub-project must find suitable premises in the right surroundings. These premises must have all the necessary rooms and functionalities. They have to fulfil all service demands (a place where everyone feels welcome and one in which it is easy to be a customer). This places demands upon the premises and choice of location. The sub-project needs to consider new work processes that can improve the efficiency in the enterprise, and special requirements for the premises. These new processes are going to utilize IT support. During the course of the sub-project, a legal and financially satisfactory contract should be signed.

On this basis the following goals for the sub-project are drawn up:

- Premises are chosen with necessary rooms and functionalities to fulfil service demands and support new and efficient work processes.
- New and efficient work processes using IT support are available.
- All necessary financial and legal agreements in connection with acquiring new premises are settled.

Based on these goals a milestone plan with three result paths is made:

- Premises (P)
- Efficient work processes (E)
- Finance and legal (F)

In the milestone plan we place Premises as the middle result path. Without underrating the other aspects of the work, this path handles the central aspect of the project. The logical dependencies between the paths make it sensible to place it in the middle to obtain a more understandable plan. The milestone plan for the example's sub-project is shown in Figure 11.4. 'Goal Director' software was used to draw the milestone plan.

The milestone plan shows the different result paths and the dependencies between the milestones. The names of the milestones are given to the right of the plan. One line is used for each milestone for the sake of both a well-arranged plan and the subsequent reports. One milestone can include several result paths. In our example we can see that in order to be able to prioritize alternative locations, they must be evaluated with respect to how the requirements for service and the opportunities for efficiency are satisfied. Consequently, the milestone includes both E2 and P6.

It is useful to study the milestone formulations. In addition to the description of the state itself, we can include conditions and requirements for achieving the milestone. Alternatively, the conditions can be drawn up as milestones in their own right. Milestone P2 says: 'Service requirements for new premises are specified on the basis of an approved mission

Milestone plan

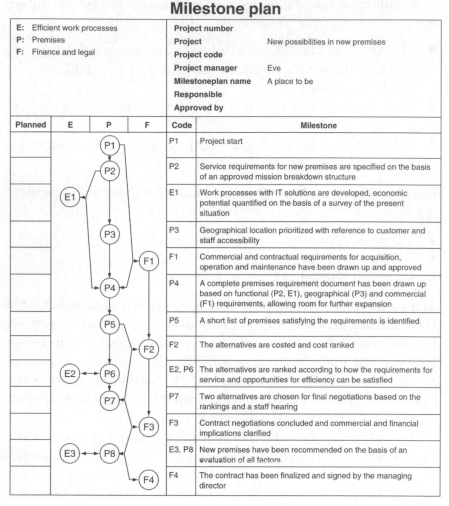

E:	Efficient work processes
P:	Premises
F:	Finance and legal

Project number	
Project	New possibilities in new premises
Project code	
Project manager	Eve
Milestoneplan name	A place to be
Responsible	
Approved by	

Planned	E	P	F	Code	Milestone
		P1		P1	Project start
		P2		P2	Service requirements for new premises are specified on the basis of an approved mission breakdown structure
	E1			E1	Work processes with IT solutions are developed, economic potential quantified on the basis of a survey of the present situation
		P3		P3	Geographical location prioritized with reference to customer and staff accessibility
			F1	F1	Commercial and contractual requirements for acquisition, operation and maintenance have been drawn up and approved
		P4		P4	A complete premises requirement document has been drawn up based on functional (P2, E1), geographical (P3) and commercial (F1) requirements, allowing room for further expansion
		P5		P5	A short list of premises satisfying the requirements is identified
			F2	F2	The alternatives are costed and cost ranked
	E2	P6		E2, P6	The alternatives are ranked according to how the requirements for service and opportunities for efficiency can be satisfied
		P7		P7	Two alternatives are chosen for final negotiations based on the rankings and a staff hearing
			F3	F3	Contract negotiations concluded and commercial and financial implications clarified
	E3	P8		E3, P8	New premises have been recommended on the basis of an evaluation of all factors
			F4	F4	The contract has been finalized and signed by the managing director

Figure 11.4 The milestone plan for the sub-project 'A place to be – new premises for efficiency and prosperity'

breakdown structure'. One uses the mission breakdown structure to get a good picture of what the requirements for the premises are. The approved mission breakdown structure could be a separate milestone. In the milestone plan we have chosen to have it as a condition in P2. The conditions put up quality standards for the work. They can refer to methods and standards. By indicating that there should be a mission breakdown structure one has made a quality demand that has to be lived up to in order for the milestone to be reached. It is important that the milestones are formulated in such a way that it is possible to ascertain that they have been reached.

Moreover, it is important that the milestone plan be complete. It should cover all aspects of the project. What we choose as checkpoints (milestones) is a question of expediency. They will reflect what we wish to focus on in the project. We have limited room, and we must weed out some milestones to obtain an easily comprehensible plan.

In the milestone plan in Figure 11.4 finish dates have not been specified for the different milestones. This is not done until the milestone responsibility chart is agreed upon and one has discussed who is in charge of achieving the different milestones. We will come back to this later.

The milestone plan contains 13 milestones (some of them located in more than one result path). Most readers of the plan would agree that it is clearly set out, even if the project tackles a difficult set of problems (finding new premises at the same time as determining what will provide improved customer service and efficiency). Dividing the plan into three result paths contributes to creating a clear overview. It would probably be possible to insert more milestones into the plan and still maintain clarity, but there is a distinct upper limit on the number of milestones that can be included.

Milestone responsibility chart

We look at the sub-project 'A place to be – new premises for efficiency and prosperity'. The milestone plan for this sub-project was presented in Figure 11.4. Figure 11.5 shows the milestone responsibility chart that responds to the milestone plan. We have once again drawn up the chart using 'Goal Director' software.

The milestone responsibility chart regulates and arranges the work to implement the milestone plan. It is important that the base organization plays a vital role in the project work. The base organization must be strongly involved for it to be possible to have better service and efficiency in the new premises. The responsibility chart must clearly indicate the roles the different parties have.

Responsibility Chart

PLAN

Project number	New possibilities in new premises
Project	
Project code	
Project manager	Eve
Milestone plan name	A place to be
Responsible	
Approved by	

X – executes the work
D – takes decision solely
d – takes decision jointly
P – manages progress

T – provides tuition on the job
C – must be consulted
I – must be informed
A – available to advise

Days: 01. Jan.00–01 May.00

RESPONSIBILITIES

Days	Start date	Finish date	No.	Milestone	Managing director 1	Head of finance 2	Head of personnel 3	Head of marketing 4	Affected line manager 5	Affected staff 6	Project manager 7	Team member operation 8	Team member financial 9	Team member legal 10	Space coordinator 11	Union representative 12	Real estate agent 13	Consultant 14
			P1	Project start														
			P2	Service requirements for new premises are specified on the basis of an approved mission breakdown structure														
			P2	Mission breakdown structure	XD	X	X	X	C	C	XP	X	I	I	I	C		T
			P2	Customer service requirements	D			Xd	d	C	XP	X	I	I	I	I		C
			E1	Work processes with IT solutions are developed, economic potential quantified on the basis of a survey of the present situation														
			E1	Develop work processes					d	X	XP	X				T		
			E1	Economic saving potential					d	C	P	X				C		A
			P3	Geographical location prioritized with reference to customer and staff accessibility	D		d	d	C		XP	X				X		

Figure 11.5 The milestone responsibility chart for the sub-project 'A place to be – new premises for efficiency and prosperity'

Ref	Activity / Deliverable	1	2	3	4	5	6	7	8	9	10	11
F1	Commercial and contractual requirements for acquisition, operation and maintenance have been drawn up and approved	D	d					–	XP	X	–	
P4	A complete premises requirement document has been drawn up based on functional (P2, E1), geographical (P3) and commercial (F1) requirements, allowing room for further expansion	D						X			–	C
P4	*Needs for rooms and space*	D				C		XP			–	
P4	*Write requirements document*	–				–		–	–	–		XP
P5	A short list of premises satisfying the requirements are identified					C		C			C	
F2	The alternatives are costed and cost ranked								XP	X		
E2 P6	The alternatives are ranked according to how the requirements for service and opportunities for efficiency can be satisfied						XP	X	C		C	
p7	Two alternatives are chosen for final negotiations based on the rankings and staff hearing	D	d	d	d	C	XP	C	C	X	C	
F3	Contract negotiations concluded and commercial and financial implications clarified	XP						x	x			C
E3 P8	New premises have been recommended on the basis of an evaluation of all factors	D	XP	C	C	–	–	–	–	C		
F4	The contract has been finalized and signed by the managing director	D	P						X			

Figure 11.5 *continued*

Special responsibilities for the heads of finance, personnel and marketing departments are stated. We also find on the responsibility chart that all affected line managers have been given an area of responsibility. The responsibility applying to the affected line managers also applies to line managers who previously have been given a defined responsibility. The special responsibilities come in addition to those applying to all those affected by the project.

Some people from the base organization will spend more time on the project than others. It is natural to talk about them as team members or project members, even if we emphasize that a formal project group has not been established. There is a need for project members who can work on customer service and operational matters. The project requires a member with expertise in economics and finance to make an economic evaluation of the alternative premises. There is also a need for legal expertise and a space coordinator. The trade union representatives have been willing to perform certain tasks beyond their role as elected representatives, so they can also be regarded as project members. It is relevant to draw some external assistance into the project. On the responsibility chart a space is allocated for a consultant and an estate agent.

Some milestones are divided on the responsibility chart because they consist of work that varies greatly in nature. This applies to P2, E1 and P4.

The different roles on the responsibility chart are shown using the symbols discussed previously. The responsibility chart should be as self-explanatory as possible. It will be all the easier to understand if those using it have participated in the development process.

Time scheduling

We illustrate the time scheduling with the completed time schedule for the project 'A place to be – new premises for efficiency and prosperity' (Figure 11.6).

One has estimated the necessary use of resources to reach the different milestones. Arriving at realistic estimates is often the most difficult part of developing a milestone responsibility chart.

In the first stage of estimating, it is the work input, not the duration or time lapse, that should be estimated. We will comment on some of the estimates in more detail to show the reasoning process:

P2 Mission breakdown structure

The management group (managing director, head of finance, head of personnel, head of marketing) and in addition the project manager and project members from customer services/operations (four people), nine people altogether, take part in a development process over two days. Thus there is a need for 18 man-days. The consultant is not included in the calculation; the time spent and the price for the person concerned is a matter of negotiation.

E1 Make new work processes

The work consists of mapping existing processes, establishing new ones, and identifying the efficiency potential. We have determined that there are 10 processes that must be described and evaluated. Each process requires a total of 1½ days and will be dealt with by a working group of an average of 3 people (different people are included in different groups). This means 10 processes × 1½ days × 3 people = 45 man-days.

P4 Space programme

The project manager will use 1 man-day and the space coordinator 8 man-days, which means 9 man-days altogether.

F2 The alternatives are calculated and ranked

The economist will use 2 man-days and the lawyer 1 man-day, which makes 3 man-days altogether.

In the resources column we have stated the total resource requirement. We could have shown the calculations to make it is easier to understand and remember the reasoning behind the resource estimates.

In this project, several of the project members have planned involvement in several project tasks. In such cases it may be necessary to draw up a workload overview for each individual member to see whether they will be able to make the desired effort. In this overview, the whole range of tasks people have

Responsibility Chart

PLAN

Project number	
Project	New possibilities in new premises
Project code	
Project manager	Eve
Milestone plan name	A place to be
Responsible	
Approved by	

Days 01. Jan.00–01 May.00

Days: 1 8 15 22 29 5 12 19 26 4 11 18 25 1 8 15 22 29

Legend:
- X – executes the work
- D – takes decision solely
- d – takes decision jointly
- P – manages progress
- T – provides tuition on the job
- C – must be consulted
- I – must be informed
- A – available to advise

RESPONSIBILITIES

No.	Milestone	Estimate (Days)	1 Managing director	2 Head of finance	3 Head of personnel	4 Head of marketing	5 Affected line manager	6 Affected staff	7 Project manager	8 Team member operation	9 Team member financial	10 Team member legal	11 Space coordinator	12 Union representative	13 Real estate agent	14 Consultant
P1	Project start															
P2	Service requirements for new premises are specified on the basis of an approved mission breakdown structure	18.0														
P2	Mission breakdown structure	5.0	XD	X	X	X	C	C	XP	X	I	I	I	C		T
P2	Customer service requirements		D			Xd	d	C	XP	X		I		I		C
E1	Work processes with IT solutions are developed, economic potential quantified on the basis of a survey of the present situation	31.0														
E1	Develop work processes						d	X	XP	X						T
E1	Economic saving potential	15.0			d		d	C	P	X				C		A
P3	Geographical location prioritized with reference to customer and staff accessibility	6.0	D		d	d	C		XP	X				X		

Figure 11.6 The time schedule for the sub-project 'A place to be – new premises for efficiency and prosperity'

Dur.	ID	Description	Responsibilities
4,0	F1	Commercial and contractual requirements for acquisition, operation and maintenance have been drawn up and approved	D d … I … XP X
	P4	A complete premises requirement document has been drawn up based on functional (P2, E1), geographical (P3) and commercial (F1) requirements, allowing room for further expansion	
9,0	P4	*Needs for rooms and space*	D C X I XP I C
1,0	P4	*Write requirements document*	I I XP I I I C
	P5	A short list of premises satisfying the requirements are identified	C C XP
3,0	F2	The alternatives are costed and cost ranked	XP XP X C
3,0	E2 / P6	The alternatives are ranked according to how the requirements for service and opportunities for efficiency can be satisfied	XP XP C C
4,0	P7	Two alternatives are chosen for final negotiations based on the rankings and a staff hearing	D d d C XP C C C X
3,0	F3	Contract negotiations concluded and commercial and financial implications clarified	XP C C X X C
0,5	E3 / P8	New premises have been recommended on the basis of an evaluation of all factors	D XP C I I I I C
0,5	F4	The contract has been finalized and signed by the managing director	D P X

103,0

Figure 11.6 *continued*

(not just implementation tasks, but also decisions and consultations, etc) must be taken into consideration.

It is necessary to look closely at the demands on the decision-makers. Will they have the time and opportunity to make the necessary decisions? We can mark milestones that require decisions with a vertical line on the time line indicating when the decision-making process should start.

After estimating the resource input, the work on the milestones will be put into calendar time. We can see from the figure that part of April is taken up with the Easter holiday and will not be used for project work. The dotted lines for some of the milestones indicate that some preliminary work has been done before the real work starts.

It is important not to draw up shorter deadlines than are necessary. For both P1 and F2 ample time is allowed for decision-making.

The activity schedule shows when the milestones are expected to be reached. The lines on the time schedule indicate the 1st, 10th and 20th of each month.

Anticipated completion dates can be entered on the milestone plan. Figure 11.7 shows the milestone plan for the sub-project (shown earlier as Figure 11.4) supplemented with the planned completion dates for the milestones.

Uncertainty analysis

At the beginning of the project, perhaps at the same time as we work on the mandate, it is advantageous to make a general uncertainty analysis. Factors for such an analysis were discussed in Figure 6.9.

After finishing the milestone plan with the anticipated completion dates, we have the basis for a more detailed uncertainty analysis. We would then look at each milestone and the related responsibilities and consider what elements of uncertainty are tied to the achievement of the milestone. The result is presented in an uncertainty matrix (Figure 11.8).

The uncertainty matrix should focus on the near-term milestones. We have the best basis to evaluate the uncertainties when work is planned to occur in the near future. It is therefore practi-

Milestoneplan

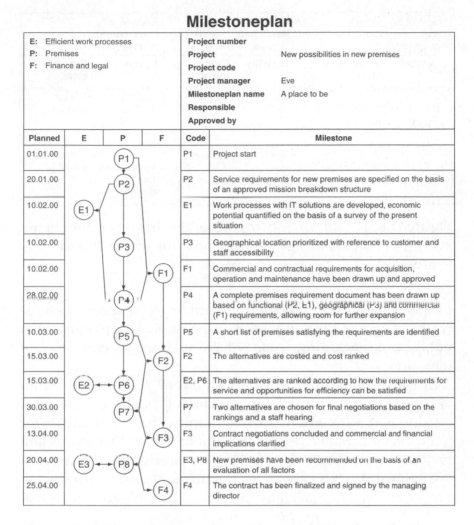

				Project number	
E:	Efficient work processes			Project	New possibilities in new premises
P:	Premises			Project code	
F:	Finance and legal			Project manager	Eve
				Milestoneplan name	A place to be
				Responsible	
				Approved by	

Planned	E	P	F	Code	Milestone
01.01.00		P1		P1	Project start
20.01.00		P2		P2	Service requirements for new premises are specified on the basis of an approved mission breakdown structure
10.02.00	E1			E1	Work processes with IT solutions are developed, economic potential quantified on the basis of a survey of the present situation
10.02.00		P3		P3	Geographical location prioritized with reference to customer and staff accessibility
10.02.00			F1	F1	Commercial and contractual requirements for acquisition, operation and maintenance have been drawn up and approved
28.02.00		P4		P4	A complete premises requirement document has been drawn up based on functional (P2, E1), geographical (P3) and commercial (F1) requirements, allowing room for further expansion
10.03.00		P5		P5	A short list of premises satisfying the requirements are identified
15.03.00			F2	F2	The alternatives are costed and cost ranked
15.03.00	E2	P6		E2, P6	The alternatives are ranked according to how the requirements for service and opportunities for efficiency can be satisfied
30.03.00		P7		P7	Two alternatives are chosen for final negotiations based on the rankings and a staff hearing
13.04.00			F3	F3	Contract negotiations concluded and commercial and financial implications clarified
20.04.00	E3	P8		E3, P8	New premises have been recommended on the basis of an evaluation of all factors
25.04.00			F4	F4	The contract has been finalized and signed by the managing director

Figure 11.7 The milestone plan with completion dates for the sub-project 'A place to be – new premises for efficiency and prosperity'

cal to postpone the consideration of milestones that are further ahead in time.

The action part is important in an uncertainty analysis. The uncertainties can be reduced through different possible measures. An uncertainty-reducing measure may cost perhaps in terms of both resources and time, but this might still be preferable because we achieve a higher level of certainty that the milestone will be reached at the anticipated time with the

Name of the project A place to be – new premises for effi- ciency and prosperity		Made by (date, name) 18.12 Project manager Eve		Approved by (date, name) 21/12 Project owner	
Milestone	**Uncertainty element**	**Probability**	**Conse-quence**	**Action**	**Respon-sible**
P2	Poor quality of mission break-down structure	Small	Medium	Training	Project manager
E1	IT resources not available	Medium	Medium	Clear commitment from IT manager	Project manager

Figure 11.8 The uncertainty matrix for the first milestones in the sub-project 'A place to be – new premises for efficiency and prosperity'

proper quality. The uncertainty matrix specifies the measures we have agreed on and who is responsible for carrying them out. Before concluding, we may have analysed several different measures.

In the example, the work on milestone P2 is based on an approved mission breakdown structure. It ought to have good quality, as it is important for determining the requirements for good service. Many people are unfamiliar with the mission breakdown structure. To ensure that developing the mission breakdown structure goes well, training is necessary. If a consultant is involved (as is already marked on the milestone responsibility chart), then some uncertainty is addressed.

Milestone E1 requires that work processes with IT support are to be developed. Activities necessary to accomplish the milestone are not considered to be particularly demanding; they will mostly be adjustments to existing processes. But there is a shortage of IT people in the organization, and it is important that they are available when the project needs them. The project owner (managing director) must have a meeting with the IT manager to make him commit himself to providing resources at the right time. Another uncertainty is addressed.

Activity responsibility chart

We look at the sub-project 'A place to be – new premises for efficiency and prosperity'. We will examine the activity planning for one milestone. We have chosen milestone E1 'Work processes with IT support are developed, profit potential quantified on the basis of a survey of the present situation'.

This is an important milestone. The project is indeed intended to lead to improved customer service and greater efficiency in the new premises. For these to be more than just fine words, the project is obliged to describe existing work processes in order to obtain a picture of the present situation. When this is obtained, a discussion must follow about what can be done better in the new premises with the integration of the previously dispersed organization. Finally, desired future work processes for the new premises must be described. The gains to be made by working in the new and improved way should also be indicated.

Figure 11.9 shows the activity responsibility chart for milestone E1. The project chooses to describe the present processes with the help of wall charts. This is a technique where an organization process is given a large-size description using actual documents to show explicitly what is going on. The project requires an external consultant to assist in this work. A clearance signal for this was given on the milestone responsibility chart. After the processes have been described, one day is set aside for a joint discussion in order to obtain a complete overview and to discuss the new solutions and processes. The work will conclude by identifying the potential for gains. When evaluating the gains, we look at opportunities for saving resources, reducing stock and wastage, and also at what will be gained through improvements in quality, which lead to more satisfied customers and greater sales.

The responsibility chart in Figure 11.9 shows the distribution of roles with the use of letters. The project has also drawn up a responsibility chart where the 'X's are replaced with estimates in man-days. This is shown in Figure 11.10. From this we can see that Eve must spend 9 man-days on the different activities in connection with milestone E1. The whole should occur over the course of three weeks, that is to say 15 elapsed working days. Others will participate with 6–7 man-days in the same period. This means that

Activity schedule

PLAN

Project number	
Project	New possibilities in new premises
Project code	
Project manager	Eve
Milestone plan name	A place to be
Responsible	
Approved by	

Days
Estimate 27.Jan.00 – 10.Feb.00

RESPONSIBILITIES

Legend:
X – executes the work
D – takes decision solely
d – takes decision jointly
P – manages progress
T – provides tuition on the job
C – must be consulted
I – must be informed
A – available to advise

Days	Start date	Finish date	No.	Activity	1 Eve (project manager)	2 Paul (sales)	3 Arthur (orders)	4 Kerstin (accounts)	5 Oscar (warehouses)	6 Thor (services)	7 Joe (purchasing)	8 William (IT)	9 Brigitte (employee rep)	10 Tom (consultant)
			E1	Work processes with IT solutions are developed, economic potential quantified on the basis of a survey of the present situation										
			E1-001	Map work processes sales	X	XP	X	X	X					T
			E1-002	Map work processes purchasing	X	X	X	X	X	X	XP	I		T
			E1-003	Map work processes service	X	X	X		X	XP	X	I		T
			E1-004	Map work processes accounts	X			XP				I		T
			E1-005	Plan 'discussion' day	XP									
			E1-006	'Discussion' day	XP	X	X	X	X	X	X	X	X	X
			E1-007	Document new processes sales	C	XP	X	C				C		A
			E1-008	Document new processes purchasing	C			C	C		XP	C		A
			E1-009	Document new processes service	C	C				XP		C		A
			E1-010	Document new processes accounts	C			XP				C		A
			E1-011	Calculate potential for gains	XP	X	X	X	X	X	X	C	C	

Figure 11.9 The activity responsibility chart for the milestone E1 in the sub-project 'A place to be – new premises for efficiency and prosperity'

Activity schedule

PLAN

Project number	New possibilities in new premises
Project	
Project code	
Project manager	Eve
Milestone plan name	A place to be
Responsible	
Approved by	

Days — Estimate 27.Jan.00 – 10.Feb.00

Days: 21 22 23 24 25 26 27 28 29 30 31 1 2 3 4 5 6 7 8 9 10

Legend:

X – executes the work
D – takes decision solely
d – takes decision jointly
P – manages progress
T – provides tuition on the job
C – must be consulted
I – must be informed
A – available to advise

RESPONSIBILITIES

No.	Activity	Days	1 Eve (project manager)	2 Paul (sales)	3 Arthur (orders)	4 Kerstin (accounts)	5 Oscar (warehouses)	6 Thor (services)	7 Joe (purchasing)	8 William (IT)	9 Brigitte (employee rep)	10 Tom (consultant)
E1	Work processes with IT solutions are developed, economic potential quantified on the basis of a survey of the present situation											
E1-001	Map work processes sales	14,0	2,0	3,0	3,0	3,0	3,0					
E1-002	Map work processes purchasing	4,0	0,5			0,5	1,0	1,0	1,0			
E1-003	Map work processes service	4,0	0,5	1,0	0,5		0,5	1,0	0,5			
E1-004	Map work processes accounts	2,0	1,0			1,0						
E1-005	Plan 'discussion' day	2,0	1,0							1,0		
E1-006	'Discussion' day	9,0	1,0	1,0	1,0	1,0	1,0	1,0	1,0	1,0	1,0	
E1-007	Document new processes sales	2,0		1,0	1,0							
E1-008	Document new processes purchasing	1,0							1,0			
E1-009	Document new processes service	1,0						1,0				
E1-010	Document new processes accounts	1,0				1,0						
E1-011	Calculate potential for gains	6,0	3,0	0,5	0,5	0,5	0,5	0,5	0,5			
		46,0	9,0	6,5	6,0	7,0	6,0	4,5	4,0	2,0	1,0	0,0

Figure 11.10 The activity responsibility chart with estimates for the milestone E1 in the sub-project 'A place to be – new premises for efficiency and prosperity'

resources than planned. We see that nothing dramatic has happened in this case, and there is really no need to report. We see that a column for revised resource estimates has been added.

Milestone plan for relocation

We will also include in this example the milestone plan for the other sub-project. The purpose of showing this plan is to demonstrate that it has a different character and distinct result paths from the milestone plan for the previous sub-project.

We do not need to wait until a contract has been concluded (milestone F4) to start planning this sub-project. It may start immediately after a recommendation has been made (E3, P8). In all probability the recommendation will be followed and we will then gain time. Obviously, however, there is the risk of wasted planning if the managing director does not approve the recommendation.

We name this sub-project 'Service, quality and teamwork in new premises'. The premises have been selected. We now wish to focus on achieving service, quality and teamwork. We do not emphasize relocation in the name. This is of secondary importance. Instead, we put the spotlight on what we want to happen in the new premises.

This sub-project has different goals and different result paths from the first sub-project. The goals are:

- Work processes and conditions for teamwork are in place, so that the organization will have the customer service and efficiency made possible by the merging and coordination of the three divisions at the new premises.
- Suitable decorated and equipped premises.
- The premises are available at the scheduled time, price and quality.
- Information to customers about the new premises, including choice of design, use of colour and signs, has been provided.

The four main goals are very general; that makes it difficult to decide if they are achieved. They should therefore be broken down into more detailed ones. Otherwise we need to add more detailed descriptions, which will become a basis for deciding if they are fulfilled.

Eve and the others must obtain genuine release and cover for their daily jobs if the responsibility chart is to be valid.

Activity report

We are following the project 'A place to be – new premises for efficiency and prosperity'. Figure 11.11 is an example of an activity report. The report was issued on 1 February and applies to activities included in the work towards milestone E1. The report is aggregated from each team member's personal report.

The project is suffering from an 'estimation error'. The resources needed for describing and evaluating the work processes were underestimated. It is not that uncommon for a wrong assessment to be made for such jobs. We can see that there were 15 processes instead of the 10 that were planned for. In addition, the seminar took an extra day. This amounts to a lot of time when nine people are involved.

To get back on course, accounting processes have been downgraded and postponed. They are not that important at this point, because they have no significance either for the choice of the new premises or for the space programme.

Milestone report

Figure 11.12 presents the milestone report for 1 March. The project has chosen to report on the 1st of every month or, when it falls on a weekend, on the last working day before the 1st.

Important results and decisions are reported. Reports are also submitted for milestones that have been started but that will be completed later. It can also be explicitly stated whether the milestone has been reached and, if so, when. This has not been done in this report.

We should always report on what is known about the final milestone. In this case it could appear that there will be a small delay. This may mean that corrective measures should be evaluated.

In addition to the milestone report, it may be relevant for the project manager to submit a report against the milestone responsibility chart, with Yes/No checks for current control criteria.

Figure 11.12 shows what a milestone report may look like as of 1 March. Once more we see that the project has used more

Activity report 27.12.99 – 30.01.00

PLAN

Project number New possibilities in new premises
Project
Project code
Project manager Eve
Milestone plan name A place to be
Responsible
Approved by
Milestone name Work processes with IT solutions are developed, etc
Milestone code

X – executes the work T – provides tuition on the job
D – takes decision solely C – must be consulted
d – takes decision jointly I – must be informed
P – manages progress A – available to advise

Activity	Estimate	Start date	Finish date	Days	Work done	Work to do	On schedule	Quality accepted	1 Eve (project manager)	2 Paul (sales)	3 Arthur (orders)	4 Kerstin (accounts)	5 Oscar (warehouses)	6 Thor (services)	7 Joe (purchasing)	8 William (IT)	9 Brigitte (employee rep)	10 Tom (consultant)
Map work processes sales	14.0	21.01.00	27.01.00		18.0		Y	Y	X	XP	X	X	X					T
Map work processes purchasing	4.0	25.01.00	27.01.00		6.0		Y	Y	X			X	X	X	XP	I		T
Map work processes service	4.0	25.01.00	27.01.00		5.0		Y	Y	X	X	X		X	XP	X	I		T
Map work processes accounts	2.0	26.01.00	27.01.00			3.0	N		X			XP	X			I		T
Plan 'discussion' day	2.0	21.01.00	28.01.00		2.0		Y		XP									
'Discussion' day	9.0	29.01.00	29.01.00		18.0		Y		XP	X	X	X	X	X	X	X	X	X
Document new processes sales	2.0	30.01.00	01.02.00		2.0	2.0	N		C	XP	X	C			X	C	X	A
Document new processes purchasing	1.0	30.01.00	01.02.00		1.0	1.0	N		C			C	C		XP	C		A
Document new processes service	1.0	30.01.00	01.02.00		1.0	1.0	N		C	C				XP	X	C		A
Document new processes accounts	1.0	30.01.00	01.02.00			2.0	Y		C		X	XP	C			C		A
Calculate potential for gains	6.0	02.02.00	10.02.00		6.0	6.0	Y		XP	X	X	X	X	X	X	C	C	
	46.0				**53.0**	**15.0**												

REPORT — Accumulated, Delay, Special problems, Waiting time, Changes required, Responsibility chart kept, Quality accepted, On schedule, Work to do, Work done

Figure 11.11 The activity report for the milestone E1 in the sub-project 'A place to be – new premises for efficiency and prosperity

Milestone report with revisions
06.03.00 – 12.03.00

E: Efficient work processes					**Project number**		
P: Premises					**Project**	New possibilities in new premises	
F: Finance and legal					**Project code**		
					Project manager	Eve	
					Milestoneplan name	A place to be	
					Responsible	Project Manager	
					Approved by	Managing Director	

Planned	Revised	E	P	F	Milestone	Reported	Report
31.12.99			P1		Project start	03.01.00	Project has started!
19.01.00			P2		Service requirements for new premises are specified on the basis of an approved mission breakdown structure	19.01.00	Milestone achieved. Mission breakdown structure and customer service requirements are approved
09.02.00	14.02.00	E1			Work processes with IT solutions are developed, economic potential quantified on the basis of a survey of the present situation	09.02.00	Required more resources and time than planned. To be reached by 15.2
09.02.00			P3		Geographical location prioritized with reference to customer and staff accessibility	09.02.00	Milestone achieved. One district given a preference. Two in reserve
09.02.00				F1	Commercial and contractual requirements for acquisition, operation and maintenance have been drawn up and approved	09.02.00	Milestone achieved. Purchase rather than lease preferred
27.02.00			P4		A complete premises requirement document has been drawn up based on functional (P2, E1), geographical (P3) and commercial (F1) requirements, allowing room for further expansion	29.02.00	Milestone achieved. Document developed and accepted by real estate agent as suitable for selection
09.03.00			P5		A short list of premises satisfying the requirements are identified		
14.03.00				F2	The alternatives are costed and cost ranked		
14.03.00		E2	P6		The alternatives are ranked according to how the requirements for service and opportunities for efficiency can be satisfied		

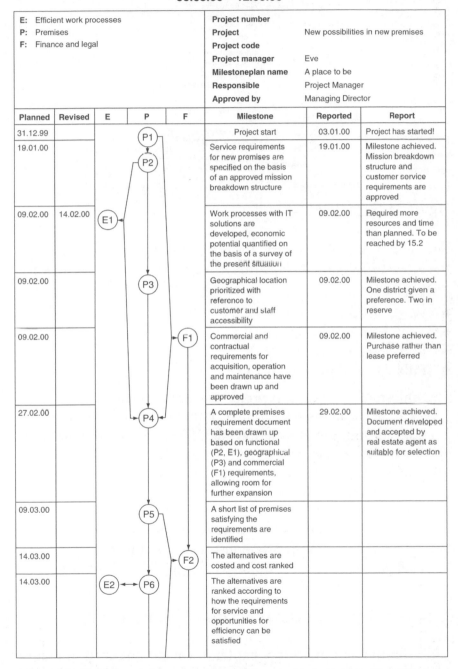

Figure 11.12 The milestone report for the sub-project 'A place to be – new premises for efficiency and prosperity'

Planned	Revised	E	P	F	Milestone	Reported	Report
29.03.00			P7		Two alternatives are chosen for final negotiations based on the rankings and a staff hearing		
12.04.00				F3	Contract negotiations concluded and commercial and financial implications clarified		
19.04.00		E3	P8		New premises have been recommended on the basis of an evaluation of all factors		
24.04.00				F4	The contract has been finalized and signed by the managing director		

Figure 11.12 *continued*

The main goals give a basis for establishing the result paths of the milestone plan. Accordingly, we have the four following result paths:

- Work processes and teamwork (WP)
- Layout of premises (LO)
- Refitting and decorating (RE)
- Publicity and printing (PP).

The milestone plan for this project is shown in Figure 11.13.

We can see from the milestone plan that milestone RE1 says that a tender for refitting is issued, while RE2 states that the premises are approved for relocation. These milestones are not sufficient to guarantee good control of the remodelling work. Therefore, refitting and equipping the premises must be managed by establishing a separate sub-project. The two milestones RE1 and RE2 will be the connection between the renovation project and the 'relocation project'. This example demonstrates that it may be necessary to detail parts of a milestone plan using separate sub-projects.

IS THE 'REQUIREMENT SPECIFICATION' FULFILLED?

After discussing pitfalls in Chapter 3, we summarized in Figure 3.6 the dangers that it is particularly important to avoid. We called this figure a requirement specification. To make it easier to read we have repeated it as Figure 11.14.

Milestone plan

W: Work processes and teamwork
L: Layout of premises
R: Refitting and decorating
P: Information and display

Project number	02
Project	New possibilities in new premises
Project code	
Project manager	Eve
Milestoneplan name	Service, quality and teamwork
Responsible	
Approved by	

Planned	W	L	R	P	Code	Milestone
				P1		Approval of design concept, including colours and graphic layout, based on two proposals from recognized designers
				P2		Contents of information programme and materials agreed upon
	W1					Physical requirements, rooms, fittings and equipment specified, on the basis of requirements for service and efficiency
		L1				Detailed facilities arrangements and layouts specified and agreed upon
			R1			Tenders sent according to practice containing a detailed remodelling programme specifying each task
	W2					Plan for training, motivation and customer management drawn up
		L2				Plans for relocation, purchasing of equipment and occupation of new premises developed and approved by those responsible
	W3					All pre-move training and education activities completed and performance evaluated according to agreed criteria
			R2			Premises approved for occupation and list of defects with amendment dates accepted by contractor
				P3		Information programme completed and printed materials produced
		L3				Kick-off activities held when the facilities are presentable after being moved into
	W4					Remaining training activities completed and further needs specified
	W5					Evaluation report on service and efficiency in new premises submitted to the managing director

Figure 11.13 The milestone plan for the sub-project 'Service, quality and teamwork in new premises'

In Chapter 3 we promised that after going through GDPM we would assess whether it satisfied the requirement specification. We will do so in this section by running briefly through our views on how the method meets the requirements. The points are stated below using keywords. The complete text appears in Figure 11.14.

- The project must work on tasks which are important to the base organization. There should be a close correlation between the direction of the company and the goals of the project
- The project must have an overview of all stakeholders and their expectations of the project
- The base organization should have principles and policies of project work
- Project methods and tools must compel those involved to spend time on defining project objectives and goals, ie what the project should achieve
- Project methods and tools must compel those involved to focus on giving the project a composite deliverable, which encompasses matters relating to people, systems (technical matters) and organization
- Project planning must take place at a minimum of two levels, the global (milestone) level and the detailed (activity) level
- Short-term, controllable intermediate goals must be set
- A plan must be clearly presented on one sheet of regularly sized paper
- Those who draw up the plans must know that they themselves will have to live with the consequences of them
- The project must have an overview of the uncertainties associated with the project and have decided how to relate to the uncertainties
- There must be an understanding of the fact that change processes take time
- There must be an understanding that a project can be organized in several different ways
- The lines of responsibility in the project must be clearly described
- Binding agreements for releasing resources for the project must be drawn up
- Line management and project members should be highly motivated
- A project manager with the right qualities must be selected
- There must be an understanding of what control is, and how important this task is in project work
- A plan must be formulated in such a way that it both facilitates and promotes control
- The project manager must be given authority in his dealing with the base organization
- Procedures for reporting must be established
- Concrete work must be done to create good conditions for cooperation in the project
- Common methods must be selected for work on the project which also encourage communication between the experts and users
- Changes in project objectives and goals must be made after careful consideration
- There must be quality control throughout the project

Figure 11.14 The 'requirement specification' (earlier shown as Figure 3.6)

Important tasks for the base organization

The use of a mission breakdown structure ensures this.

Overview of stakeholders

The use of stakeholder analysis ensures this.

Principles and policies for project work

The principle responsibility chart establishes the central principles for decision-making authority, communication, participation and division of work in the project.

Precise definition of the project's goals

Use of mandate with purpose and goals ensures this. The milestone plan, with its result paths, requires goals to be defined precisely. Without goals it is impossible to set up a good milestone plan.

Focusing on composite goals

A PSO test of the main goals ensures this. It is also taken care of when the milestone plan has several result paths, which show that the project should produce several types of results.

Layered planning

This is one of the strongest points of the method. Planning (and control) occurs at both global and detail levels.

Short-term controllable intermediate goals

The milestones in the milestone plan serve this function.

Clear plans

The milestone plan is presented on one page. Use of standardized forms provides the framework for a clear presentation of the whole project.

The planner must live with the plan

The responsibility charts clarify responsibility relationships. We have stressed that those who will perform an activity must participate in planning it.

Overview of uncertainties

The use of uncertainty analysis ensures this.

Understanding that change takes time

The method does not have much to offer here, but division into several result paths in the milestone plan, with the opportunity to focus on human adjustment and development, provides more realistic planning of the human change processes.

Understanding control

We do not guarantee that the method will provide a deeper understanding of control, but the simple and manageable reporting procedures following certain control criteria should facilitate control.

The plans promote and facilitate control

This is a strong point of the method. The control criteria are defined precisely on plan and report forms. Conditions are correctly set up for individual reports and meaningful control.

Project manager with authority in the line

The principle responsibility chart and the milestone responsibility chart define precisely the terms of responsibility and authority, but this method cannot guarantee that everyone will live up to what is described and agreed upon. The formal agreement makes it easier to follow up if the line is not meeting its commitments.

Established pattern of communication

Reporting is formalized. In addition, we have stressed that the deeper report dialogue should be structured and not 'idle chatter'.

Understanding that there are different ways of organizing a project

The responsibility chart promotes a discussion of different ways of dividing work tasks and decisions in a project. The discussion shows that people are free to organize themselves in many different ways.

Clear descriptions of responsibility in the project

Again a strong point of the method. The responsibility chart clarifies terms of responsibility. These are precise and difficult to run from.

Binding agreements on releasing resources

The milestone responsibility chart is such a binding agreement.

Motivated line manager and project members

This is a matter that the method does not specifically deal with, though probably the overview and the clear agreements required by the method, and clarity of reporting and control, will aid motivation.

Correct choice of project manager

This is an area where that method does not make a significant contribution. The method starts when the project manager has been chosen.

Good cooperation in the project

This is an area that is not covered explicitly by the method. It is an important area, and methods to improve cooperation in the project should be drawn from elsewhere. We believe that clear areas of responsibility and authority are a good basis on which to build cooperation.

Methods that promote communication between users and experts

Detail planning is formalized through an activity responsibility chart. Specific methods are described that are important with reference to both time scheduling and resource estimation. The project management method in itself does not require or stimulate use of particular methods in the professional work.

Changes in goals after careful consideration

The responsibility charts define precisely who can decide on changed goals.

Quality control along the way

The milestones make it possible to check that the project is progressing according to plan. We have stressed that the milestones should be formulated such that they facilitate quality control.

FINAL COMMENTS

We have now presented GDPM. We went through principles that are important for planning, organizing and controlling projects. We have shown that GDPM is a comprehensive method that builds on these principles.

The method requires an ability to think logically and systematically throughout a project and to describe precisely what has been agreed upon. Certain forms support it and discipline the work to make it easier to follow the method. However, there are few forms, so that the work does not become unduly complex.

The method is IT supported by Goal Director software. It guides you in the work of making plans and reports, helps you reduce mistakes, and therefore gives you more time for the real planning work of logical thinking and precision.

A project that follows GDPM substantially improves its chances of being a successful project. However, we have also underlined the significance of the project culture for the results. Therefore, it is necessary to include a reminder of this by way of conclusion. The organization must work constantly on improving its project culture. We suggested a comprehensive and systematic projectivity programme.

Even if you do not start such a programme, you can improve the project culture in the base organization.

We therefore wish to point out four areas that everyone should work on in order to improve the chances for successful projects.

The base organization must demonstrate that it wants to manage its projects

A minimum for a project management policy is that management agrees that all projects over a certain size and complexity should be planned and organized with the aid of a milestone plan and responsibility charts.

The base organization must demonstrate that it is concerned with the progress of its projects

Projects should submit a milestone report to the managing director (or another person in top management, if this is more appropriate) on the first day of every month.

The base organization must increase the professional prestige of project management

Project management must be regarded as a distinct profession demanding great expertise and long experience. An organization can only afford to have a limited number of people with the necessary qualifications; therefore it must select workers with good organizational experience as project managers. Young, inexperienced people are too lightweight. You must invest in people who are willing to be project managers, and who do not see this as only a short episode, a stepping-stone to line management.

The base organization must make use of its own project experience and constantly develop project expertise

It is desirable that project managers have their own forum with fixed meeting times, for example the last working day of each month. Examination of project reports and discussions of new plans, with the aim of improving quality, should be permanent agenda items at such meetings. Discussing common problems must be a central point. The most usual themes will be lack of resources, slow decision-making processes, difficulties in prioritization, and reprioritization.

Sources

Chapter 1 Introduction

As you have experienced, this book is not a general book on project management. It does not cover all possible project topics. Instead, it presents a well-proven project management method for planning, organizing and controlling projects. It is a method developed and used by the authors themselves.

There are a lot of good books on project management in general. We especially recommend some of the books by J Rodney Turner (Turner, 1999; Turner and Simister, 2000). They are broader in their approach, but are advocating the same thinking and methods as they are based on the first edition of this book. Among the American textbooks we point to Kerzner (2003) and Meredith and Mantel (2000).

Our book focuses on PSO projects. The authors developed this concept. There are also other authors who have stressed that a successful change process should consist of a composite approach. Leavitt's Diamond has most metaphorically expressed this thinking (Leavitt, 1965). The corners of his diamond illustrate that tasks, (organizational) structure, technology and people are intimately knitted together. If there are changes to one of these components, the others will be affected. This is exactly the same as is expressed by PSO.

Chapter 2 Project characteristics

This chapter is about what a project is and describes a project by the most common characteristics. There are many definitions of a project.

PMI (Project Management Institute) is the largest member association in the world within project management. It now has more than 100,000 members from all over the world. Its Web site is: www.pmi.org. PMI has issued a standard for project work, which is considered by many to be a de facto standard for the project management profession (PMI, 2000). It is called PMBoK® (A Guide to the Project Management Body of Knowledge). This type of standard may tend to be somewhat conservative and is not always capable of adapting quickly to new thinking. Our book contains thoughts that have not yet been implemented in PMBoK®. However, PMBoK® is valuable reference in many instances. It defines a project in the following way: 'A project is a temporary endeavor undertaken to create a unique product or service.'

There are also other bodies of knowledge, well worth looking into, like those of APM (Association for Project Management, Web site www.apm.org.uk/) (APM, 2000) and IPMA (International Project Management Association, Web site www.ipma.ch/) (Caupin, Knöpfel, Morris and Pannenbäcker, 1999). In the UK the project management methodology PRINCE 2 has gained prominence as the de facto standard in many instances (OGC, 2002). OGC stands for Office of Government Commerce.

The PMBoK® definition has been criticized for not addressing the single most important aspect of the project. 'The Scandinavian School of Project Management' stresses the organizational perspective and says that a project should be looked upon as a temporary organization that is established to carry out a certain task (Lundin and Söderholm, 1995). The Scandinavian approach to project management is presented in a comprehensive manner in Sahlin-Andersson and Söderholm (2002).

A quite new definition covers the many aspects of a project (Turner and Müller, 2003): 'A project is a temporary organization to which resources are assigned to undertake a unique, novel and transient endeavour managing the inherent uncertainty and need for integration in order to deliver beneficial objectives of change.'

Chapter 3 Pitfalls in project management

There are many presentations of project failures. The most well known is probably that of Kharbanda and Pinto (1996). A newer book that discusses large projects is by Flyvbjerg, Bruzelius and Rothengatter (2003). Failures within IT projects have been extensively researched (Ewusi-Mensah, 1997).

However, there is consolation – some success stories exist (Laufer and Hoffman, 2000).

Chapter 4 Foundation of the project

If a project is to be a success, it must have a clear purpose and clearly stated goals. Many authors have discussed this part of the foundation of a project (Atkinson, 1999; Baccarini, 1999; Lim and Mohamed, 1999; Munns and Bjeirmi, 1996; Pinto and Slevin, 1988; Turner, 2002; Wateridge, 1998).

We recommend that a mission breakdown structure is developed in order to express clearly the responsibilities of the project. The authors developed this tool to be part of the project methodology. A similar approach can be found in Frame (1995); see especially Chapter 4 'Making certain the project is based on a clear need'.

We also recommend that a stakeholder analysis is conducted (Cleland, 1988b; McElroy and Mills, 2000).

We argue vigorously for the use of responsibility charts. This is a well-known method within project management that is traditionally used to express the responsibilities of the team members for carrying out the different tasks of the project (Cleland and King, 1988). We have extended the use of responsibility charts beyond the traditional way and use them to express division of responsibilities between the project and the base organization (the principle responsibility chart) and responsibilities for achieving the milestones (milestone responsibility chart).

Chapter 5 Global planning – milestone planning

The milestone plan is the core element of our project methodology. A more theoretical reasoning behind the approach is given in Andersen (1996).

Chapter 6 Global organizing – milestone responsibility chart

For PSO projects we recommend a matrix organization. This means that project team members work simultaneously for the project and the base organization. Many discuss the different ways of organizing projects and their strengths and weaknesses (Dinsmore, 1984; Gobeli and Larson, 1987; McCollum and Sherman, 1993).

When discussing organizing, it is an advantage to distinguish between external organizing (organizing the relationships between the project and the base organization) and internal organizing (organizing the relationships between the project manager and his team members). This is done in Andersen (2000), which builds on Frame (1995), especially Chapter 3 'Structuring project teams and building cohesiveness'.

When the project has drawn up the milestone plan with planned dates, we recommend that an uncertainty analysis be carried out. The most extensive presentation of uncertainty analysis is by Chapman and Ward (1997). Recently they have made some changes to their terminology (Ward and Chapman, 2003).

Chapter 7 Detail planning and detail organization

Our detail planning and organization is tied to the activity responsibility chart. In large and middle-sized projects, network planning will be of great help. There are many textbooks covering the subject. A thorough book is the one by Lockyer and Gordon (1996).

Chapter 8 Project control

This chapter demonstrates how a project can be monitored, both on the detail level (activity level) and on the global level (milestone level). More detailed techniques than the ones we use to control the progress of the project are available, for example earned value (Fleming and Koppelman, 2000).

It might also be of interest to carry out a project health check. This will give an overall picture of the 'health' of the project. Tools (usually questionnaires) are available to do such a check (Andersen and Jessen, 2000; Grude, Turner and Wateridge, 1996; Pinto and Slevin, 1987; Slevin and Pinto, 1987).

In this chapter we cite Brooks' Law, which says that in general it is dangerous to add more people to your project if it is delayed. His project experiences are related in Brooks (1995).

Chapter 9 Quality in project work

We have emphasized the importance of quality control. We have guidelines that can be used to secure quality. Other approaches may also be of interest. The organization may make use of the international quality standard for project work drawn up by the International Organization for Standardization (ISO, 1997) or the more general guidelines of the European Foundation for Quality Management (EFQM) applied to project management (Westerveld, 2002).

Chapter 10 Project culture

This chapter accentuates the significance of creating an appropriate organizational culture within the project. The importance of this was pointed out early on (Cleland, 1988a; Elmes and Wilemon, 1988; Firth and Krut, 1991). It is possible for the project to check and evaluate its own organizational culture (Andersen, 2003).

The project approach to work requires a new type of management, new institutions and new roles to be filled (Turner and Keegan, 1999). The challenges are particularly large for the project manager. It is of the utmost importance to find a person who is able to do the job (El-Sabaa, 2001; Hauschildt, Keim and Medcof, 2000).

We recommend a projectivity programme for the organization to better its organizational culture. The Swede Torbjörn Wenell invented the word 'projectivity' (Wenell, 2001).

Chapter 11 Goal Directed Project Management – example and summary

The chapter gives an example of the use of the methodology. We have used the IT software Goal Director. Today, it is necessary to have good IT support during the planning and control of a project. The software should be selected after careful consideration (Aaron, 2002).

References

Aaron, A L (2002) A systematic methodology for selecting project management systems, *AACE International Transactions*, IT11

Andersen, E S (1996) Warning: activity planning is hazardous to your project's health! *International Journal of Project Management*, **14** (2), pp 89–94

Andersen, E S (2000) Managing organization – structure and responsibilities, in *Gower handbook of project management*, 3rd edition, ed S J Simister, pp 277–292, Gower, Aldershot

Andersen, E S (2003) Understanding your project organization's character, *Project Management Journal*, **34** (4), pp 4–11

Andersen, E S and Jessen, S A (2000) Project evaluation scheme, *Project Management*, **6** (1), pp 61–69

APM (2000) *Project Management Body of Knowledge*, Association for Project Management, High Wycombe

Atkinson, R (1999) Project management: cost, time and quality, two best guesses and a phenomenon, it's time to accept other success criteria, *International Journal of Project Management*, **17** (6), pp 337–342

Baccarini, D (1999) The logical framework method for defining project success, *Project Management Journal*, **30** (4), pp 25–32

Brooks, F P (1995) *The mythical man-month: essays on software engineering*, Anniversary edition, Addison-Wesley, Reading, MA

Caupin, G, Knöpfel, H, Morris, P W G and Pannenbäcker, O (1999) *IPMA Competence Baseline, Version 2.0*, International Project Management Association, Zurich

Chapman, C and Ward, S (1997) *Project risk management: processes, techniques and insights*, John Wiley and Sons, Chichester

Cleland, D I (1988a) The cultural ambience of project management – another look, *Project Management Journal*, **19** (3), pp 49–56

Cleland, D I (1988b) Project stakeholder management, in *Project management handbook*, ed W R King, pp 275–301, Van Nostrand Reinhold, New York

Cleland, D I and King, W R (1988) Linear responsibility charts in project management, in *Project management handbook*, ed W R King, pp 374–373, Van Nostrand Reinhold, New York

Dinsmore, P C (1984) Whys and why-nots of matrix management, in *Matrix management systems handbook*, ed D I Cleland, pp 394–411, Van Nostrand Reinhold, New York

Elmes, M and Wilemon, D (1988) Organizational culture and project leadership effectiveness, *Project Management Journal*, **19** (4), pp 54–63

El-Sabaa, S (2001) The skills and career path of an effective project manager, *International Journal of Project Management*, **19** (1), pp 1–7

Ewusi-Mensah, K (1997) Critical issues in abandoned information systems projects, *Communications of the ACM*, **40** (9 September), pp 74–80

Firth, G and Krut, R (1991) Introducing a project management culture, *European Management Journal*, **9** (4), pp 437–443

Fleming, Q W and Koppelman, J M (2000) *Earned value project management*, 2nd edition, Project Management Institute, Upper Dalby, PA

Flyvbjerg, B, Bruzelius, N and Rothengatter, W (2003) *Megaprojects and risk. An anatomy of ambition*, Cambridge University Press, Cambridge

Frame, J D (1995) *Managing projects in organizations: how to make the best use of time, techniques, and people*, revised edition, Jossey-Bass, San Francisco, CA

Gobeli, D H and Larson, E W (1987) Relative effectiveness of different project structures, *Project Management Journal*, **18** (2), pp 81–85

Grude, K V, Turner, J R and Wateridge, J (1996) Project health checks, in *The project manager as change agent*, ed L Thurloway, pp 204–224, McGraw-Hill, London

Hauschildt, J, Keim, G and Medcof, J W (2000) Realistic criteria for project manager selection and development, *Project Management Journal*, **31** (3), pp 23–32

ISO (1997) *Quality management – Guidelines to quality in project management* (ISO 10.006), International Organization for Standardization, Geneva

Kerzner, H (2003) *Project management: a systems approach to planning, scheduling, and controlling*, 8th edition, John Wiley and Sons, New York

Kharbanda, O P and Pinto, J K (1996) *What made Gertie gallop? Lessons from project failures*, Van Nostrand Reinhold, New York

Laufer, A and Hoffman, E J (2000) *Project management success stories: lessons of project leaders*, John Wiley and Sons, New York

Leavitt, H J (1965) Applied organizational change in industry: structural, technological and humanistic approaches, in *Handbook of organizations*, ed J G March, Rand McNally, Chicago

Lim, C S and Mohamed, M Z (1999) Criteria of project success: an exploratory re-examination, *International Journal of Project Management*, **17** (4), pp 243–248

Lockyer, K and Gordon, J (1996) *Project management and project network techniques*, 6th edition, Pitman, London

Lundin, R A and Söderholm, A (1995) A theory of the temporary organization, *Scandinavian Journal of Management*, **11** (4), pp 437–455

McCollum, J K and Sherman, J D (1993) The matrix structure: bane or benefit to high tech organizations? *Project Management Journal*, **14** (2), pp 23–26

McElroy, B and Mills, C (2000) Managing stakeholders, In *Gower handbook of project management*, ed S J Simister, pp 757–776, Gower, Aldershot

Meredith, J R and Mantel, S J, Jr (2000) *Project management. A managerial approach*, 4th edition, John Wiley and Sons, New York

Munns, A K and Bjeirmi, B F (1996) The role of project management in achieving success, *International Journal of Project Management*, **14** (2), pp 81–87

OGC (2002) *Managing successful projects with PRINCE 2*, third edition, The Stationery Office, London

Pinto, J K and Slevin, D P (1987) Critical factors in successful project implementation, *IEEE Transactions on Engineering Management*, **34** (1), pp 22–27

Pinto, J K and Slevin, D P (1988) Project success: definitions and measurement techniques, *Project Management Journal*, **19** (1), pp 67–71

PMI (2000) *A Guide to the Project Management Body of Knowledge*, Project Management Institute, Newton Square, PA

Sahlin-Andersson, K and Söderholm, A (eds) (2002) *Beyond project management. New perspectives on the temporary – permanent dilemma*, Liber Ekonomi, Malmö, Sweden

Slevin, D P and Pinto, J K (1987) Balancing strategy and tactics in project implementation, *Sloan Management Review*, **29** (1), pp 33–41

Turner, J R (1999) *The handbook of project-based management: improving the processes for achieving strategic objectives*, 2nd edition, McGraw-Hill, London

Turner, J R (2002) Project success criteria, in *Project management pathways*, ed M Stevens, Association for Project Management, High Wycombe

Turner, J R and Keegan, A (1999) The versatile project-based organization: governance and operational control, *European Management Journal*, **17** (3), pp 296–309

Turner, J R and Müller, R (2003) On the nature of the project as a temporary organization, *International Journal of Project Management*, **21** (1), pp 1–8

Turner, J R and Simister, S J (eds) (2000) *Gower handbook of project management*, 3rd edition, Gower, Aldershot

Ward, S and Chapman, C (2003) Transforming project risk management into project uncertainty management, *International Journal of Project Management*, **21** (2), pp 97–106

Wateridge, J (1998) How can IS/IT projects be measured for success? *International Journal of Project Management*, **16** (1), pp 59–63

Wenell, T (2001) *Wenell om projekt* (in Swedish: *Wenell on project*), Uppsala Publishing House, Uppsala

Westerveld, E (2002) *The Project Excellence Model: a concept linking success criteria and critical success factors*, paper presented at the IRNOP 5, Rotterdam

Index

Figures in the text are in *italics*

The Handbook of Project Management
A Practical Guide to Effective Policies and Procedures
Second Edition
Trevor Young

"A practical, comprehensive guide to be used frequently."
EURONET

Project management skills are hugely desirable for managers at all levels of an organization. Most people today can benefit from the application of these skills to some areas of their daily operations. From large undertakings, such as the Channel Tunnel or North Sea oil rigs, to the unique but smaHacktorpller projects that take place in every type of organization, special skills are required if project management is to produce the right results.

This fully updated second edition of *The Handbook of Project Management* is written specifically to help project managers improve their performance using tried and tested techniques. It will be particularly useful if you are: looking to develop project management skills; starting a new project; wishing to acquire new skills; or training others in project management skills.

The Handbook of Project Management second edition now includes:

- programme management;
- the relationship betwcen programmes and projects;
- new ideas and opportunities for programmes and projects;
- a free CD ROM containing a collection of tools and presentation materials that support the methodology used in the book.

Packed with concepts and processes, tools and presentation materials, this comprehensive handbook will assist anyone who is responsible for converting strategy into reality.

The Practice of Project Management
A Guide to the Business-Focused Approach
Enzo Frigenti and Dennis Comninos

"This comprehensive title will assist anyone who is responsible for converting strategy into reality."
European Foundation for Management Development

In today's highly competitive and fast-paced environment, the rapid creation and delivery of high-quality products and services is critical to business survival. To meet these demands, modern businesses need to operate at high performance levels, harnessing the full power of their resources to focus on strategic and business objectives, and deliver business benefits.

Traditional project management has tended to focus primarily on the processes of managing projects to successful completion. To manage projects from their inception through to actual delivery of the business enabling objectives, a different project management approach is needed. Project management needs to become part of the business and, in order to achieve this, organizations need to come to terms with the business of project management.

This book addresses the concepts and issues of business project management. It aims to assist organizations in making the shift from a narrow, strong, technical focus on project management to a broader, more business-oriented focus. *The Practice of Project Management* introduces three basic concepts which underpin the philosophy of the business-focused approach:

- Business Focused Project Management (BFPM™);
- The Wrappers™ model;
- Objective Directed Project Management (ODPM™).

Packed with unique concepts, processes and models, this comprehensive title will assist anyone who is responsible for converting strategy into reality. It will also enable the development of project management skills to complement technical expertise, and allow readers to provide the project skills their customers demand.

Successful Project Management
Apply Tried and Tested Techniques, Develop Effective PM Skills and Plan, Implement and Evaluate
Trevor L Young

Project management has become an area of interest in all types of organization and the skills required are recognized as highly desirable at all levels. The role of project manager requires maintaining a balance between the demands of the customer, project, team and the organization. This provides a real challenge in the fields of time management and prioritization.

Successful Project Management will enable any manager to significantly increase their projects' chances of success and contains practical and well-tested techniques. This step-by-step guide will help you with:

- project conception and start-up;
- managing project stakeholders;
- managing risks;

- project planning;
- project launch and execution;
- closure and evaluation.

Complete with checklists and specific guidance notes, this essential book covers the entire project management process and will help you get the results you need.

Advanced Project Management
A Complete Guide to the Key Models, Processes and Techniques
Alan D Orr

Project management has become one of the most valued skills in business: to thrive, it is essential that companies deliver their projects on time. Companies depend on the expertise of skilled project managers; and major projects require project managers with advanced skills.

To move from intermediate to advanced project management, a project manager must understand not only the project itself but the overall needs of the company. They must also know how to build and manage teams, how to handle large budgets, and appreciate the difference between gathering information for managing the project, and gathering information for managing the stakeholders.

This book explains these skills, setting out processes, methods and tools to enable a project manager to handle the greater volume of requirements and change that occurs in complex projects.

Contents include:

- getting started;
- estimating time-scales and budgets;
- moving from macro to micro planning;
- team building;
- executing the project;
- project control;
- closing the project;
- rescuing a failing project.

The above titles are available from all good bookshops. To obtain further information, please contact the publisher at the address below:

Kogan Page Limited
120 Pentonville Road
London N1 9JN
United Kingdom
Tel: +44 (0) 20 7278 0433
Fax: +44 (0) 20 7837 6348
www.kogan-page.co.uk